I Know the Psychology of Rats

First published in India in 2023 by
Tulika Books
44 (first floor), Shahpur Jat, New Delhi 110 049, India
tulikabooks.in

ISBN: 978-81-956392-0-5

Design: Alpana Khare
Printed at Lustra Print Process Pvt. Ltd., New Delhi

I Know the Psychology of Rats

Saeed Mirza

illustrated/designed by
Nachiket Patwardhan

Tulika Books

Contents

CHAPTER 1

Did he really say it?

It was 1987 and when I heard the story, I thought to myself ... it was crazy and damned funny, but did he really say it? I turned to the assistant director.

"Are you sure ...?"

"In front of me ... he said it in front of Ravi and me."

Ravi was our man Friday. I probed some more.

"Did something provoke him?"

"It was a rat, a real rat that ducked below the office cupboard ... we created a racket, so it ran into the store room. Ravi and I followed. A little later he entered and said, relax ... he'd handle it. He had a large broom in his hands."

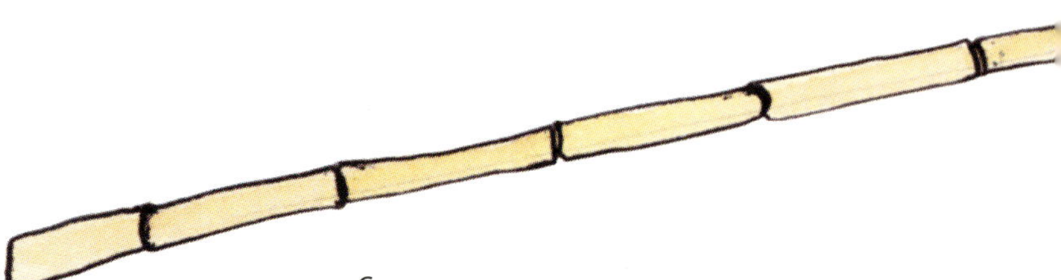

"That must have looked damned funny."

The assistant nodded and decided to dramatize the event.

"It was. He was holding it as if it were a club and carefully checking the floor behind the discarded junk in the corner. I wonder if he thought he was some kind of warrior. If he did, how would he use this makeshift weapon in this tiny store room? Then he carefully surveyed the junk and walked around it and peered into the darkness between it and the wall and murmured –
'Son of a bitch ... if he thinks he's smart, I'm smarter.'"

"He said that too?"

The assistant nodded again and continued.

"Suddenly the rat emerged from under the rubble and he jumped in fright. Ravi kicked it against the wall and knocked it out, then picked it up by the tail and left. And then he said –
'I knew he would emerge from this side.'
So I asked him, how did you know that?"

"And that's when he said it?"

"Yes."

I burst out laughing.

"The guy is nuts", I said.

CHAPTER 2

The Guy

'The guy' was a film-maker who was famous for his frenzied shooting style. His continuous takes and retakes of a shot, his exasperating method of covering a scene from almost every angle, his habit of shooting so many scenes that quite a few would get left out in the editing room – all this so exhausted his cast and crew that very often they would fall asleep on the set while he wondered why they were so tired.

He started his film career by making one masterpiece of a film. It was a hilarious comedy with political and social overtones, and later he followed it up with another incredibly innovative and funny love story. Then he entered mainstream cinema and made a passionately felt film about a young woman battling for her rights as a patriarchal society tried to make her conform to its rules. The film was just modestly successful and he was disappointed.

"I hope I am not doomed to keep doing funny stuff."

It seems that was what his backers wanted

What followed next was a series of mainstream films that were situational comedies but you could tell his heart was not in it. They were financial failures and one was not even released. And with each failure he would condole with his producer and refuse to take the rest of his fee. That did not help and by this time he was fast losing out on backers who still believed in him.

"What they want, I don't. What I want, they don't."

Finally, he changed track completely. No more funny. No more cuteness. He would get to reality in a completely new way ... his way.

His first attempt was a film based on a true story. It was the horrifying tale of three sisters who had committed suicide together in a town in North India. They had made a secret pact to relieve their lower middle-class parents of the humiliation of finding them husbands, which they knew would be heart-breaking. It was a story that millions of poor and middle-class families face, and his approach to the subject was stark, almost ascetic, a complete change from anything he had ever done.

The film did not work with audiences.

He was depressed for a while, then recovered and began furiously working on fresh scripts and ideas. He would scrap some, chop and change others, rewrite some others. And then write some more fresh ideas. The files stacked up in his cupboard bore testimony to all that activity.

Somebody joked, "He has enough material to shoot for the next twenty years."

Then, in 2012, five years after the last disaster, a producer did arrive and backed his final effort: a film that combined politics, the theatre of the absurd, and a bizarre narrative where a whore is manipulated to enter politics and her gradual understanding about the nature of power and how ordinary citizens are brutalized and used as cannon fodder. Some of the jokes and characters were embarrassingly lewd and at times surreal. The film shocked most of his friends. The others did not know how to respond ... nor did his producer.

"Why such graphic imagery?" someone finally asked.
"It's the truth ... isn't this really the state of affairs in our country? Why hide it?" was his reply.

The film got a deliberately tepid release and later a friend would shake his head and sadly whisper: "He's lost it."
Maybe he had, but his writing did not stop. He went on an almost manic journey to script more ideas that he hoped one day would turn into films. It didn't happen that way.

On the television front he was the maker of a series of path-breaking and hugely popular programmes. That did not satisfy him.
"I know they are popular ... but why do programmes have to be only funny? Why the hell are we imitating American shows?"

I thought he had a point.

He now moved to a series on a police station and used this opportunity to hammer home some hard 'truths' about Indian society. The series was painstakingly well-researched and scripted, well-directed, the performances of the actors balanced and professional. And the net result was a programme that powerfully revealed the brutal nature of the state and the dehumanized system of law enforcement. His message was clear: There is very little justice for the poor and the disenfranchised in the land.

It jolted the authorities and was summarily banned. There would be no review. Our man was genuinely surprised:
"Why did the bastards ban it? I'm going to Delhi to fight my case."

Later, the authorities relented and a watered-down, much milder version was found acceptable to which he reluctantly agreed, but he was deeply disturbed. Yes, when he dealt with what he felt was the truth, he would go all the way.

Now, some questions need to be asked. When did he start believing that this form of artistic construction, of seeing reality through a distorted magnifying glass, was the perfect way to reflect the world as he perceived it?

If one looked carefully, perhaps there were some signals: the gradual shift in the kind of books that he was reading, his intense response to Indian and world political affairs, his passionate debates about the role of art, his changing views on the aesthetics of cinema, and finally, his fascination with the political stance and form of the Stanley Kubrick film *Dr. Strangelove*.

He must have gone through a tumultuous upheaval.

It was this journey that would force him to carry the guilt of the incredibly violent 2002 Gujarat communal riots, in which hundreds of Muslims were slaughtered, on his tortured shoulders, even though he had nothing to do with it.

"I am a Gujarati and a Hindu, aren't I?" was his terse comment. "Someone has to take the responsibility."

I could not believe it. Was he serious? When I looked at him again, I knew he meant it.

He was also a man who started out thinking all Marxists were assholes and ended up being more Marxist than Karl Marx – a man who loved Charles Chaplin and Buster Keaton, Truffaut, Hitchcock, Guru Dutt, Bimal Roy and Satyajit Ray – who, surprisingly, loved reading James Hadley Chase and Saadat Hasan Manto along with Dostoevsky, Kafka and Bulgakov, Premchand, Gorky, Tolstoy and Chekhov. His reading list was endless. Later he would move to non-fiction with a huge emphasis on political essays, biographies, screenplays, and books on history and art.

But it was Dostoevsky who dominated his mind and his soul.
"He is the only writer who really understands the pain of human existence."

Books books and more books.

He bought them from stores, off the streets, in towns and cities across the country, spending a minor fortune building up a personal library. How the hell could one explain this? How could a man who was so embarrassingly cost-conscious, almost stingy, be so bloody extravagant? It didn't make sense.

But, buy he did.

One day many years later, perhaps out of guilt, he quietly informed me that sometimes, just sometimes, he would take a couple of books out of a store without paying for them.

"How often?" I asked.

"Twice', he said sheepishly. "It was in the early days. I didn't have the money, but I wanted those books. Plus, it was in England ... the bastards had looted us so I did a bit of recovery. Don't look at me like that.'

The man would later hate George Bush for the Iraq War and other US presidents for "heaping shit on the world", Narendra Modi the Prime Minister of India for his continuous lying and bigoted governance, and would finally, and passionately, come to believe that the world was actually run by a cabal of secretive and manipulative bankers and financial warlords who kept the planet in a state of perpetual conflict and upheaval. As far as China was concerned, he was figuring out a way to figure it out. He was also a man who loved *pani* and *sev puri, batata wadas* with a lot of chilli powder, was strictly a vegetarian at home and very, very non-vegetarian outside.

"You think I'm a schizophrenic?"

And finally, a man who would one day announce that he believed he was of Scythian stock because he had read somewhere that many of the people of Gujarat and Sindh had that ancestry.

What?!

Here he was, a short dark man, in the most painfully ordinary shirt and trousers, wearing the most painfully ordinary glasses, believing that he belonged to the race of those ancient and fierce, horse-riding nomadic warriors of the Central Asian steppes who were the scourge of civilizations. It required some imagination. Later, he further announced that he looked more like a clerk than a film director. That assessment was much closer to the truth.

Yes, he was the man who I thought was an unimaginative workaholic when I first met him at the Film School in Pune in 1973, who I later came to accept and finally respect after I saw his final year diploma film. He would become my friend, partner and close confidante, and his name was Kundan Shah. He was the one who, in 1987, said:

"I know the psychology of rats."

Maybe he did ... who knows?

Kundan Shah died on the 7th of October, 2017.

Kundan Shah died on the
7th of October, 2017.

Soliloquy 1

Why am I
writing this book?
Is it because
I feel
it is necessary
and my time is
running out?
Perhaps that is true.
It is becoming
more and more difficult
to remember
the conversations, camaraderie,
intellectual debates and dialectical
upheavals with a friend.
Then I think:
Will all of this make sense to my readers?
What are they going to make of it?
I don't know, but I have to get this off my chest.
I have to present this wonderful,
crazy and vulnerable friend of mine to the world
because he deserves it,
and also because I firmly believe,
he had not "lost it".

In fact towards the end of his life his more and more surreal, bizarre and sometimes viciously crude representations of reality came so much closer to the sordid 'truth' of our times that it was embarrassing to quite a few of his friends and admirers. Was it because they saw their own acquiescence to this state of affairs difficult to stomach?

Perhaps.

I also hope the reader will find the book interesting despite its social and political stance, because there is a story in it ... a story of a deeply passionate Indian and world citizen. A citizen who, by using humour, the absurd and the grotesque, attempted to unravel our times and the world we have inherited.

I say this because I believe he had reached a point in his journey which forced him to strip away the frills and facades of our reality and see it for what it really was, its essence: compassionless, grotesque, with moments of beauty.

That was the way he saw it ... not just India but the world.

It was not pretty – it was bleak ... gloomy ... amoral yet starkly poetic ... and, at times, ironic and excruciatingly funny. In fact each failure seemed to push him to further extremes till his final film, which was a political metaphor about our scoundrel times. Yes, the film was deeply flawed, but was his grotesque representation of our political reality very far from the truth?

The short and unassuming man in glasses who looked more like a clerk than a film-maker had been through a tumultuous journey, and, I believe, it is a journey worth revealing. He attempted to unmask the 'big lie' that all of us have to live to accept the political, economic and social circumstances we find ourselves in. In a strange way, I also believe he was born to be inflicted with pain because he could no longer be just a film-maker – and this is his story.

It is also a story about two people who could not have been more different from each other and who, over time and circumstance, built an incredibly strong bond of trust and friendship. You could even call them 'comrades': Kundan Shah and I, Saeed Akhtar Mirza.

This book is our perception of the world we have all inherited.

Snippet

"Did you see him pouring out tea to Obama?"

"Yes ... that was symbolic."

"Yeah, and cute ... our humble Prime Minister serving tea to the most powerful man in the world – Indian hospitality, and all our television cameras recording it for the whole country to see. The cameras are always around when his mother feeds him, when he washes the feet of the poor, when he meditates alone in a cave ... they are always around."

"Full marks to his media strategists ... the press laps it up and then they tell the people of the country to lap it up."

"Yeah ... repeat those images ... not just once but a thousand times. It all seems so easy running a country ... **just bring in the f*****g cameras**."

I laughed.

It was in the first few days at the film school that I noticed him

CHAPTER 3

It was in the first few days at the film school that I noticed him. I had no choice. He was different and a bit irritating. I remember wondering what kind of film-maker he would be when all he did was take down notes in the classroom. Did he ever actually listen to what was being said ...?

Even at film screenings, pen and pad in hand, he would furiously jot down notes. What the hell could he see in the dark? Could he even see what he was writing?

Later, much later, he explained: "I was noting down entries and exits ... camera angles ... checking for continuity jerks ..."

What?!

Writing all that stuff in a dark theatre? Couldn't he just watch the bloody film and take it all in and then figure out entries and exits and other details on the editing table? This was getting ridiculous. And it lasted for three whole months ... at every screening in class and after class, which could mean four films a day ... two shorts ... a documentary ... and a feature. It seemed he couldn't trust his mind ... he had to put everything down on paper. And soon he had a couple of disciples – they did the same thing and it drove the rest of us crazy. We called them the 'gang of three'.

However, he was in a class by himself. Two tales will explain how:

The tale of the Patriot

It must have been a month after we joined film school and the 'ragging' season wasn't really over. 'Freshers' would still be singled out for entertainment and what better bait would a senior want than 'the gang of three'.

One day, as we were emerging from the Main Theatre after a night screening, we saw the 'gang' standing around the flag-post outside the Director's office, saluting an imaginary flag high above and singing the national anthem. It seems that some seniors had cornered them as they left the theatre and ordered them to do so.

Students stopped by and observed the three tuneless and patriotic singers of the night. They found it hilarious ... but the story does not end there.

As soon as the national anthem was over, Kundan switched over to an impromptu and tuneless ode to a writer that he admired. The students were surprised and amused. Then he switched to another ode to a favourite film-maker as he and his friends continued to stand at attention and salute the sky. The students now applauded.

The 'gang' completed their act, bowed to their audience, and walked back to their hostel rooms.

The tale of the 'Kamikaze' Owl

When we were in the middle of our first year at film school, the students began to notice something very peculiar. After the night screening, as the boys were returning to their hostel rooms, on a dark patch of road between two street lights, they were being attacked by an owl that would swoop down from the trees. The owl would fly close to the head, sometimes even clip it with a wing, and fly away.

This went on for two weeks and it drove the students crazy. They would cover their heads with their hands and make a dash across those twenty-five deadly yards.

What the hell was happening? It was Kundan who finally had an explanation for it.

"I have studied the situation carefully", he said.

"And what have you found?" someone asked.

"The owl is only attacking guys who don't wear glasses. Someone without glasses must have provoked that owl and now he is getting his revenge."

"Bullshit!"

"You don't have to believe me."

"Okay, if it's true, why the hell are you running too?"

"I don't want to take any chances."

It was funny. But. Had he really made that study? Luckily for Kundan, the attacks stopped and the owl disappeared. Later someone said he had actually seen Kundan standing late at night outside the classroom theatre, which was at the other end of the deadly stretch, observing the students as they ducked and ran.

Was that true?

"I wouldn't put it past him", someone muttered. "He's the only guy I know who would do it."

That was the kind of reputation he built up in just six months. He was the 'forensics' man.

Besides, there were other little details
that caught our attention:
though the 'gang' did participate
in reviews and analyses of films
and theory with the rest of us,
we realized they just listened
to what we were saying
and their 'real' discussions and debates
were with each other.
Not that we really minded,
but we wondered why
they didn't open up with us.

"How can every film be political?"

"Because every genre,
even entertainment represents a world view ..."

"Even entertainment?"

"Yes. Look at most of the stuff
emerging from Hollywood ...
does it really reflect American reality?"

"Is it supposed to?
Why can't you just have fun ... relax?"

"Isn't that a world view?
Just relax ... have fun ...
don't think about your life ..."

"Can't you just enjoy a bloody film
without getting into all this shit!
You are putting labels on people
that even they are not aware of."

Maybe arguments like this kept them away.
Then there was the insidious bit.

Early one morning, a batch member going to the common washrooms noticed 'the gang of three' heading towards the editing room. He was surprised and when he checked the time, it was 5 in the morning. The event was duly reported to the rest of us. The same thing happened the next day ... and the next.

What were they up to?

A normal day ended at around 11 at night after the feature film screening, and then students would go back to their rooms to discuss the film. This mostly lasted about an hour, but it was rumoured that the 'gang' discussed things for longer. So when it was found out that they were heading to the editing room every day at 5 in the morning, it set us thinking.

How much sleep were they getting ... were they sleeping at all ...?

It was finally revealed that they had got special permission to view film prints from the archives on the editing table – and they were doing it without telling the rest of the class. In other words, extra 'special' classes so that they could study films in close-up.

"Sneaky bastards", some of us muttered.

The so-called 'sneaky bastards' were getting just about three hours of sleep every night for an entire semester so that they could get that extra edge over the rest of us, and we wondered why. Years later, the many mysteries were unravelled to me by the man himself.

"What f*****g extra edge?" he yelled angrily.

"You guys gave us such a complex ... your confidence in asking questions in class, your easy facility with the English language, just the way you guys walked and talked, dealt with the women on campus, gave us a complex."

"It took just two days for me to feel somehow inadequate. Then there were your discussions on politics – socialism, Marxism, the Naxalite movement in India, the Vietnam War, liberation movements in Africa ... it had us foxed ... it had me foxed."

"What did all of this have to do with cinema? Added to all of this were those underground films from Latin America and all those fiery discussions and debates. In just the first week I knew I had a lot of catching up to do. That was when I began taking down notes, on everything ... editing, film theory, lenses and cameras. I was going to suck out everything that was available for me to learn from."

"Do you know why I felt this way? Let me tell you. I come from a trading family ... my father was a small-time dealer in Aden. For generations we've been small-time traders. Do you know what that means? It means a narrow, tunnelled mind ... f*****g fixed ... eternal. I wanted to break free. I loved to read books, any kind of trash that came my way ... and I loved to go to the cinema – these were my two passions."

"After graduating in India with some kind of education I needed a job – in our family everyone has to contribute in some way ... remember, we were seven children and I the eldest son. So I got a job, but not the kind my family expected. It was in a small but well-known book shop that gave me access to vernacular literature. It didn't pay too well but the owner was a great man who knew that I was hungry ... to learn, to do something different with my life."

"That was when I decided to join the film school. I had saved up some money and I studied hard for the entrance exam ... and I made it. I was elated. I had just about enough resources for the first year, therefore I desperately needed a scholarship to see me through."

"And when I come to the film school, what do I see? I see confident guys and girls taking about philosophy and art and music, as if they were born into it. They also seemed to have no real problem with finances, while I had to count every bloody rupee to make sure I didn't run out of money. These confident people were not the majority ... but they gave the rest of us a complex."

"That's why I began taking down notes. I listened to you guys discuss cinema with all those fancy words ... but I did not have the courage to speak up and express my point of view. That's why whenever we had free time we went to the library to read. I read books on editing and cinematography, on screenplay writing ... my head was spinning in trying to catch up, and I was also constantly worrying about money that would cover my expenses. I was not looking for an extra edge ... I was trying to catch up like a madman."

"And here is another secret ... our so-called 'gang' thought that the rest of you were politicizing everything, including cinema. What the hell did Marx or any other political thinker have to do with cinema? Left wing, right wing, liberal, fascist, anarchic ... some of you guys reduced everything to a world view and so many students got roped into those debates. We didn't come to film school for that ... we saw cinema as something different."

"That's why we kept away from most of you ... we did not want to be contaminated. It was only in our final year that we began to understand your point of view, and you began to understand ours."

He paused for a moment and then added,
"Now I smile when I think about that time ... today I f*****g see politics everywhere."

It was, I think, 1989 when it all came out, just like that – the revelation. It was thirteen years since we had graduated from film school, and by then Kundan and I were partners.

... we both had come a long way

... and that passionate and eloquent outburst taught me a lot.

That outburst of Kundan in 1989 revealed a lot of other lessons that had to be learnt. How had I not read the signs that he had talked about? Most of the voluble 'visible lefties' at film school came from a certain background: they were from elite schools and colleges, were English-speaking, and exuded a casual confidence in social relationships. They talked about justice and equality, discussed wars and liberation movements, debated about history, aesthetics and art with confidence, and yet spoke in a language far removed from the rest of the students. Besides, they dealt with ideas for their intrinsic value rather than through lived experience. How the hell then could they reach out to the rest of the students?

Did they even attempt to?

But the argument went far beyond our campus. It would extend to the world at large as social and political activists attempted to identify with and fight for the causes of the underprivileged, the unequal and the disenfranchised. They would have to realize that it was not good enough to talk about ideas, change and philosophy ... what was also important was the language in which these were conveyed. As someone said:

"... history is littered with the corpses of good intentions."

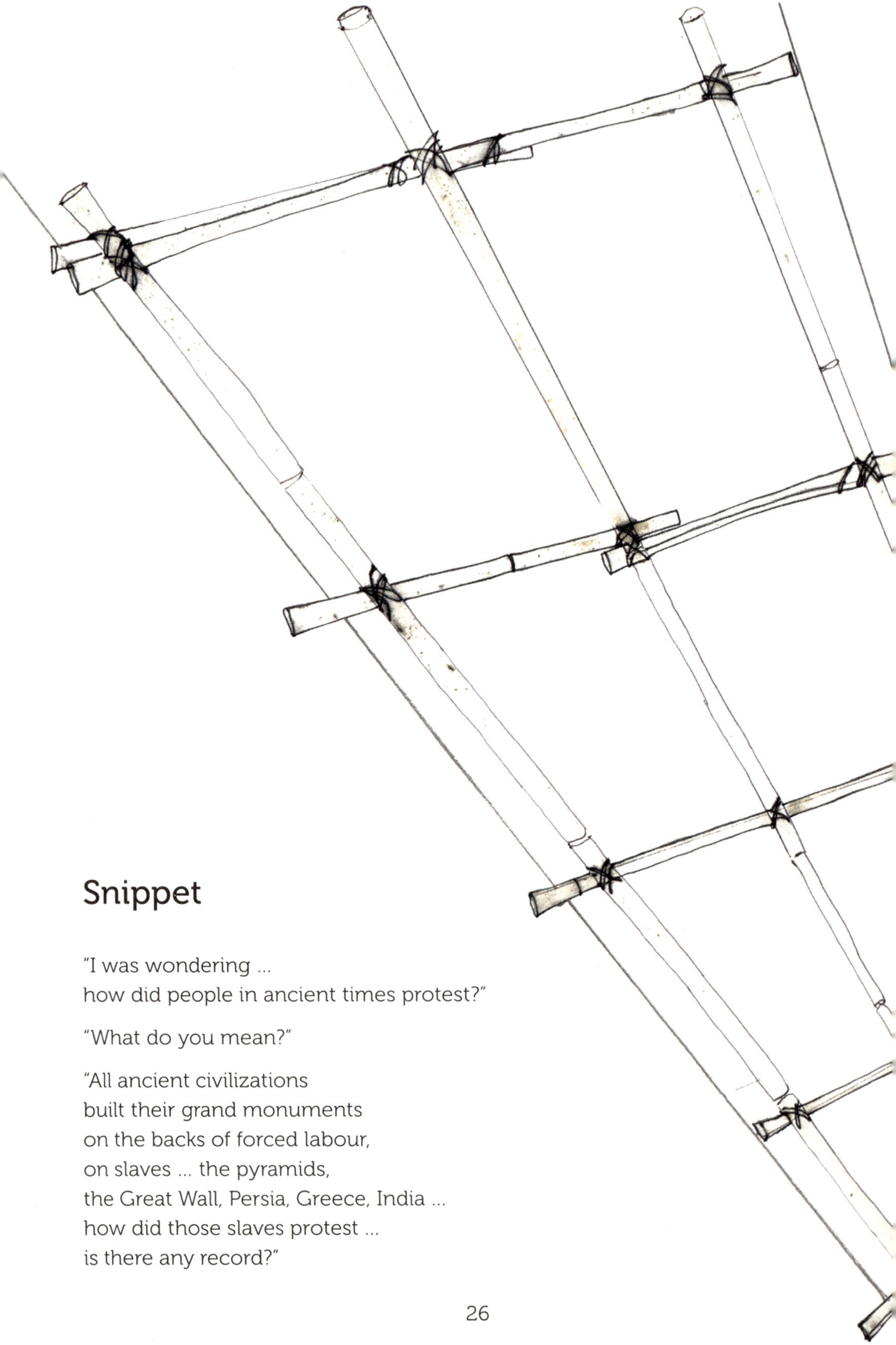

Snippet

"I was wondering ...
how did people in ancient times protest?"

"What do you mean?"

"All ancient civilizations
built their grand monuments
on the backs of forced labour,
on slaves ... the pyramids,
the Great Wall, Persia, Greece, India ...
how did those slaves protest ...
is there any record?"

"I don't know.
Why are you thinking about this now?"

"The apartment building in front of ours is being painted ...
there was some kind of makeshift scaffolding ...
and I used to watch those workers paint ...
no safety net, no nothing ...
and yesterday morning one of them slipped
and fell from the seventh floor.
He landed head first on the concrete road."

"What?!"

"Yes, head first ...

slave labour of our civilization ...
wonder where he was from ...
his family ..."

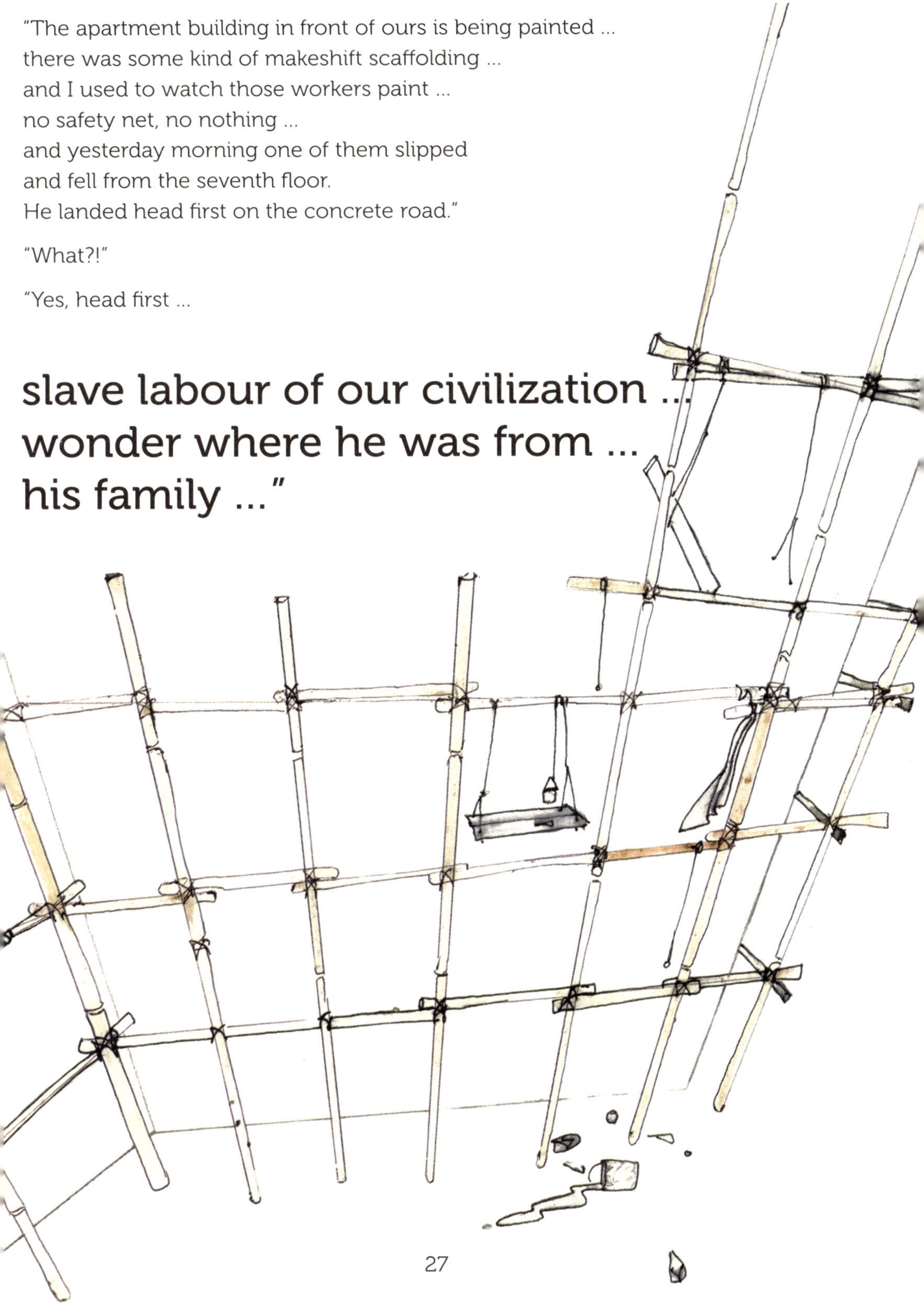

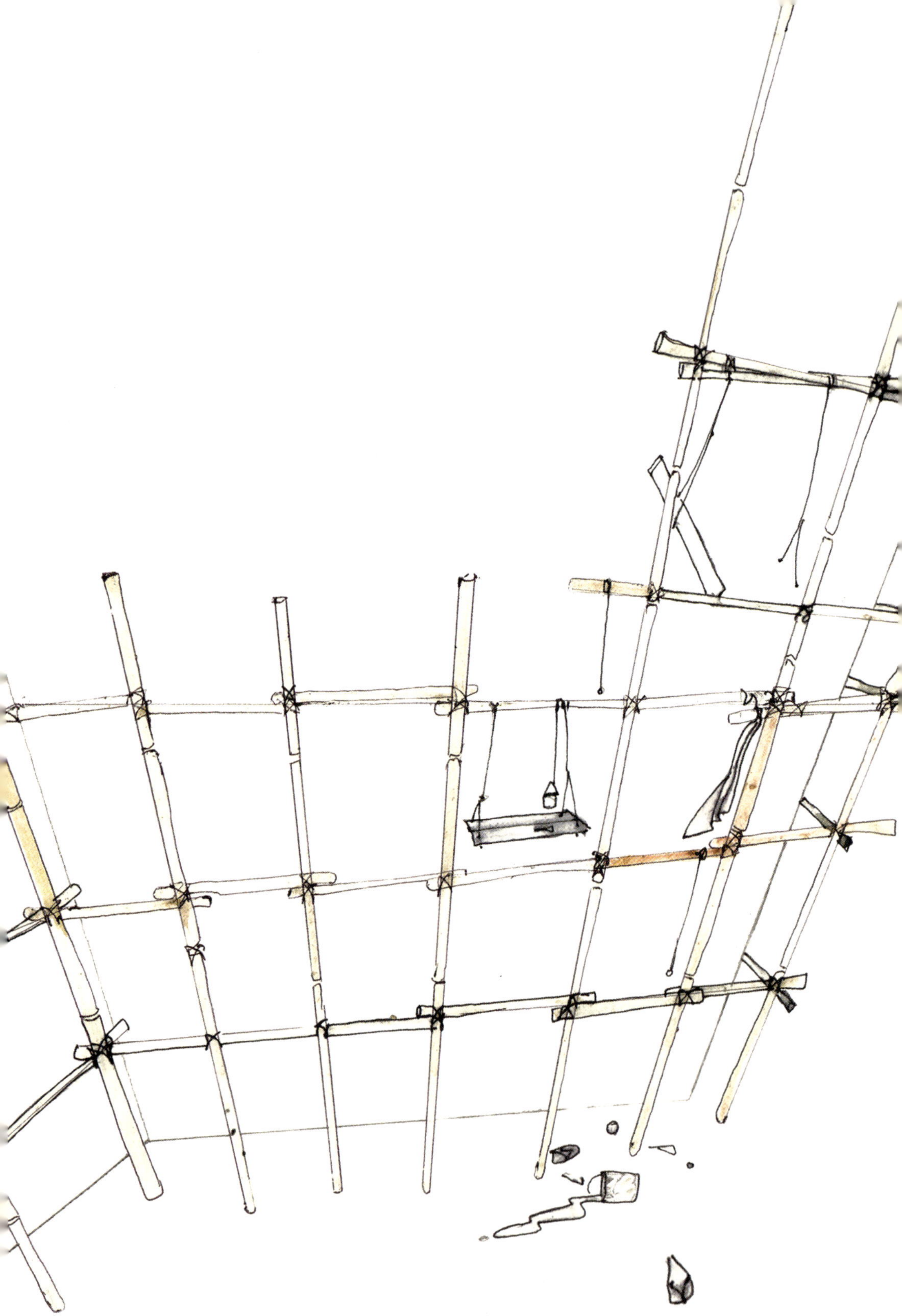

Argumentative Indians

"Can't you guys see a film just as a film ... nothing more?" Kundan asked.

It was the end of the year 1974 at film school, and the answer to the question came swiftly from Hari of the famed 'lefties'.

"I can't, and I will tell you why. There is no act of creation in isolation. The tragedy with you guys is that you think we see things mechanically, but it is not true. We believe that there is enough space in art for both intuition and deliberate consciousness. And that is what makes great art. You cannot be ignorant about what's happening in your own life and in the world and pretend it does not matter because you want to be a 'pure' artist. There is no such thing."

"How would you slot **Dostoevsky**?"
"I have not read enough of him."
"That, precisely, is your problem."

Film school was a battleground: for heated debates, arguments and, once in a while, even assaults.

It was crazy, but true. If you examined the background of the authors, the creators of the cinema that the students viewed in the classrooms and theatres on campus and discussed under the Wisdom Tree, what else would you expect?

These people were not just film-makers ... they were 'agents provocateurs', people with 'hidden agendas'.

Let me tell you about them.

They were entertainers, philosophers, inventors, comedians, magicians, anarchists, dreamers, Marxists, humanists, painters, architects, adventurers, dropouts, ethnographers, poets, writers, even fascists. All of them iconoclasts and the cinema that they created came in all styles, shapes and forms.

These were the early masters who were pushing the language and grammar of the medium to new frontiers. And, this was the cinema that was being viewed and slowly being understood and digested by the students. The two words that can best describe these times are: memorable and exhilarating.

There were other factors too that added fuel to the debates.

Remember, I am talking of the late 1960s onwards when there were so many liberation movements occurring in Africa and Latin America, and Vietnam had become the greatest rallying point for anti-war activists around the world. The French, the Brits, the Dutch and the Spanish were having a rough time maintaining their empires. The Americans were seeing revolts in their backyard, in Latin America.

In India too there were insurrections and upheavals in the north of the country as indigenous tribal people and the poor picked up arms against the state in the heartland. They were branded as 'Naxalites'. In the north-east there were other armed insurrections. Another storm was brewing in the country as students, farmers and railway workers organized mass protest movements against the government's policies.

It was an age of revolts, resistance and discovery, and the students at the film school had ringside seats to witness this changing world order.

Latin American cinema provided them a glimpse of the tumultuous times across that continent with films from Brazil, Argentina, Chile and Mexico. The films from Cuba celebrated the revolution. French, Italian, Spanish, Swedish and German cinema was awash with new ways of seeing both life and art after the horrors of the Second World War. Even smug Switzerland produced some gems. Then there was cinema that emerged from those devastated lands of Eastern Europe: from Poland, Czechoslovakia and Yugoslavia, from Hungary and Russia.

In all of this I still remember the one time when there was no debate, just complete consensus ... when our entire batch came together to celebrate a silent film made in 1921. It was called *Man with a Movie Camera*, made by Dziga Vertov, a Russian director. As we emerged from the classroom theatre it was Kundan who started the eulogy:

"What a film ... he was like a child having so much fun, discovering the moving image, playing games ... cinema for the sake of cinema."

Other batchmates joined in.

"Yeah ... as Griffiths and Edison are trying to tell stories, as Eisenstein is trying to formulate theories, and Phalke planning mythologicals ... this guy is just having a ball, and telling us to do the same."

"Just take the camera and shoot."

"Yeah ... liberation ... freedom ..."

But the feast didn't end there.

For the first time the students were also seeing and experiencing cinema from other parts of India. It was a cinema that went beyond the boundaries of popular entertainment and brought in a whole new way of looking at reality. Leading the charge was cinema from Bengal, Kerala, Andhra and, surprisingly, Hindi cinema that was taking on the mighty Bombay film industry. And, quite a few film-makers in the vanguard of this movement were from our film school.

This wave would rapidly spread across the country and lead to further debates.
"Why don't you just let Guru Dutt and Bimal Roy be? Theirs might not be 'New Wave' cinema but they did reveal an Indian reality."
"Of course they did ... I was just trying to say that it was a kind of middle-of-the-road cinema that led to the New Wave. Why do you guys get so excited?"
"Because we too like the New Wave ... but we don't dismiss popular cinema."
"We don't either."
"Thank you for being so kind."

Adding to the flavour were gems that emerged from countries like Iran, Tunisia, Turkey, Egypt and Nigeria, from Japan, Korea and China. It was a never-ending viewing of short films, features, documentaries and experimental cinema from around the world, and the students were relishing it.

Sometimes questions were posed.
"Are we are seeing enough of popular cinema? Isn't that also necessary?"
The questions were valid ... and they were also on the minds of most students.
And the answer was simple: we were not. The students knew that too, despite the occasional screenings of Hollywood blockbusters.

However, they also knew that when they finally left the film school, all that they would get would be 'popular cinema' from the big studios of Hollywood, Mumbai and Chennai. This school was providing them with an alternative way of seeing.

It was an opportunity and they grabbed it.
And it showed in their work.

I'll tell you how.
It did not matter whether you were a student director, cinematographer, sound engineer or editor, your work was beginning to see remarkable change. It was turning nuanced, at times, subliminal. For students of the screenplay writing and acting course it was another kind of exposure from the standard mainstream fare that emerged from Hollywood or studios in Bombay, Madras and Calcutta. If this did not cause debate, what would? I would call it the 'great churning'.

Ideas, stories and aesthetics

were being debated ... form and content were being analysed

Most importantly,

the students were beginning to discover themselves ...

... and finding paths on which they could travel.

"I don't think great literature can become great cinema", Kundan announced one day.

"Why do you say that?"

"Can you really capture the nuances of a great novel? You can't. Cinema needs to create its own stories ... cinematic stories. If you want to use literature, use some trashy stuff."

He was countered.

"That's what Godard said too ... but I don't agree with him."

"Why?"

"What about Ray's trilogy ... cinema and literature?"

"That's what I mean ... that is an example."

"What?!"

Kundan hadn't realized he had almost blasphemed. It was a miracle he was not thrashed by the lovers of Bengali literature and lucky for him that he quickly clarified his comment:

"I mean, that is the rare exception."

The opposition calmed down.

CHAPTER 4

A Houseboat in Kashmir

It is late night in July 2021 and here I am sitting on the patio of a houseboat in Kashmir on the Dal Lake and I shall pretend that everything is normal in this forsaken land. That's what houseboats are for, aren't they ... to help you forget?

So, I shall wish away the more than thirty years of unbelievable violence and despair the people here have witnessed. For the Kashmiri Hindus, a traumatic exodus. For the Muslims, a horrifying exodus as well as an existential experience. I shall also forget that Kashmir is now no longer a state but a Union Territory, and is ruled by a man appointed by the central government and not by elected representatives.

This was achieved by ramming through a bill in Parliament in faraway Delhi without really asking the people living here. They were given no choice. I still remember seeing the elated parliamentarians celebrating on television channels. They thumped their desks, hugged each other and shouted slogans about "history being created and a promise fulfilled". Some even shed tears of joy. The scenes were ecstatic.

I wonder what Kundan would have to say about this? A lot, I bet.

As far as those parliamentarians are concerned, they had every right to be elated because they had kept their word. This abrogation of the special status was clearly stated in the manifesto of their party, and the bill was passed through a massive show of hands and thunderous 'ayes'. A promise was fulfilled. It did not matter to them that they had just overturned a sovereign commitment to the people of Kashmir that granted the state a special status. And since most Kashmiris were Muslim anyway ... could they really be trusted?

So, what can I say? Was the bill passed democratically? It was. Was it really democratic? It wasn't. Yes, democracy can be ugly too. So, I shall talk about other things.

Beyond the lake in front me is a hill on top of which is an ancient Shiva temple, which, legend claims, was built by the renowned Hindu scholar and saint Adi Shankaracharya. He was the man who, legend once again claims, was responsible for the revival of the Vedic faith in India. A faith that was renowned for its tolerance, non-violence and philosophical sweep.

I decide to study this history later.

My thoughts now turn to the worldwide Covid crisis and the immense tragedy that it spawned in my country right at the initial stages.

As word about the virus spread, as news about what steps nations were taking to prevent it spread, my country decided to be in the forefront of this war and my decisive leader decided to show the world what real 'leadership' meant. So, he gave the entire nation of 1 billion and 300 million people just four hours to prepare for a complete lockdown. They would have to stay home indefinitely as the country would shut down completely ... no buses, no trains, no aircraft, no automobiles, no anything. Only emergency personnel and services would be allowed to function.

What the great leader in his designer clothes and in his quest to prove how decisive he could be did not realize was that his country was substantially run on the backs of slave labour: approximately 200 million people who were migrant workers and daily-wage earners, the luckiest of whom had moved a few miles from their villages to the nearest small town in search of work. The others, approximately 40 million, were the unlucky ones. They had left their homes and had travelled hundreds of miles, sometimes more than a thousand, to the big towns and cities, hoping that some day they would get the opportunity that could change their future. All of them lived in makeshift accommodations. Hovels, really.

How would these millions of people reach their distant homes?

It was shocking and tragic to see them attempt to return as some television crews began to record this devastating and brutal migration. There were these millions upon millions of desperate people. Walking. Cycling. Endlessly. Mile after tortuous mile. Entire families of men, women and children. Trying to get home anyway ... anyhow. It was perhaps the worst the world has ever seen. Within a frenzied fortnight of heart-breaking stories these images suddenly disappeared from television screens and newspapers.

Suddenly. Just like that. Was this disappearance calculated? It looked like it because those images were being seen in middle-class and upper-middle-class homes, the core constituency and supporters of the regime. And those images were not very pretty ... in fact they were ghastly.

How many among these desperate multitudes reached their homes ... and how? The country will never know. But, as is the case with most such memories, this migration of the disenfranchised will soon be forgotten. The great leader will remain unscathed. So I must get back to the pandemic.

What is this virus?

It was supposed to be a slightly more vicious variant of the ordinary 'flu', but it turned out to be completely different. It is continuously mutating and millions of people have died around the world, and in its 'democratic', universal sweep it has spared no one: rich or poor, black, brown or white, Christian, Muslim, Hindu, Buddnist or atheist. As we slowly recover from the global trauma, another world has quietly emerged.

It is the world of isolation.

We are afraid of meeting each other, talking to each other, hugging and debating, protesting or just being with each other. The message is clear, stay at home if you want to be safe. Just follow the rules about masks, vaccines and social distancing. Listen to the doctors and experts on your television sets, mainstream media and mobile phones, and pray that they and the political leaders are right. Because, quite honestly, no one knows what is really happening and everyone is shooting in the dark. There are newer and newer strains of the virus emerging and there is a constant reminder of a looming threat on the horizon.

Is this the future? If it is, for how long will it be?

FOREVER?

Forever is a long time and I, not really a hero, dislike such terms. So I have been travelling, with all precautions, to places, and meeting friends and generally conducting my life as normally as I possibly can. Like I said, I am not a hero but I honestly feel that a world cocooned under such circumstances is like a manufactured coma. Am I anti-science? I know I can never be ... but human beings have over time become incredibly creative social animals, and to deny them that capacity to think together, laugh and debate together, is a crime.

The silence is deafening.

I take a pause and look at the Kashmiri night sky,

and this is when I think of Kundan once again.

I reflect about a conversation I had with him years ago. Yes, it almost seems that these are the perfect times and conditions for the powerful and secretive 'cabal' that he had talked about. It seems our 'Covid' era of isolation and segregation has delivered them a bonanza, and I smile as I recall that conversation ... it was quite bizarre.

Let me tell you that story.

Ever since our work slowed down, which means from around 2008 onwards, Kundan and I would meet regularly for a drink or two about once a fortnight. When I say a drink or two it could also mean three or four with a makeshift meal tossed in. The meeting could be either in his office or my house, which were literally 200 yards from each other. We would talk about a lot of things but the real concentration would be on recent political events in India or anywhere else in the world. If the subject was international, you could bet that the role of the United States would take centre stage.

And this time, once again it was.

I think it was around the middle of 2009 and Barack Obama had been recently sworn in as President of the USA. Our discussion centred around two issues. Would he really be able to change US foreign policy and try to remedy, in some form, the havoc and destruction his country had created in Afghanistan and Iraq? Would he really be able to confront the forces that had created the economic and financial crash of 2008, which had led to such despair among the poor across the world?

Kundan's position was clear on both counts. It did not matter that Obama was African American ... it did not matter whether he was pink, white, purple or blue ... nothing would change.

"The US needs wars, it needs constant enemies ... and when old ones disappear, they create new ones."

"That military machine has to be continuously fed ... there are too many big players who have created this machine and have stakes in it. So there has to be a constant imagined threat and therefore constant vigilance. And why do we have to be vigilant? Because freedom is at stake. What a wonderful word to use: freedom! It always resonates with people ... while no one asks, 'whose freedom?'"

As I listened to Kundan, I agreed with much that he said ... yes, there was this massive, endlessly hungry war machine, but there were also important people in the US government who recognized it for what it was, and there were hundreds of thousands, millions of ordinary American citizens who were also against these wars. Didn't that count? Couldn't Obama tap into this constituency? Besides, I had heard some of the speeches he had made as a young, up-and-coming politico ... the man seemed different.

Kundan shook his head.

"Look what he has done with all those banks during this financial mess. He has bailed them out. He has bailed out all the big bastards who created this crisis. Did the American people want that? Every survey showed that they did not."

As the conversation got heated and the whiskey flowed, Kundan suddenly fell silent. He raised his hand and gestured to me to pause. Then he said:

"Follow me ... I want to show you something."

He walked to the balcony of my apartment and looked up at the sky.

It was around 11 pm
and it was dark.
I looked up too.
There was nothing to see, not even the stars.

"What do you see?" Kundan asked.
"I can't see a thing."
"I know. But there is a lot happening out there
and that is the secret the world needs to know."

He took a deep breath and began to speak.

"So, let me tell you about this dark sky where you cannot see a thing. Not just this dark sky but dark skies around the world. Right now there is a lot of electronic and digital money being sent across those skies to all kinds of destinations ... stock exchanges, into banks, also into safe havens. Frankfurt ... London ... Shanghai ... New York ... Tokyo: trillions upon trillions of dollars of legitimate and illegitimate money. This is the world of finance."

"Quite a bit of it is the loot of money launderers, drug dealers, speculators in stocks and shares, manipulators of commodities and their prices, arms dealers funding deadly insurrections, money looted from countries by dictators, robber barons, politicians or just plain thugs. Then there is the illicit money from casinos and other forms of gambling and the re-routing of funds from the underworld everywhere. All of it will be made 'respectable' by sharp money manipulators."

"Then there is the legitimate money being wired by the big corporates: the arms industry, the food and pharmaceutical cartels, the mining and mineral cartels, the commodities cartels, the chemicals and oil corporates, the big trading houses. All this is happening in that dark sky: the loot and the legitimate ... all part of the great capitalist system."

Kundan now turned to look at me.

"And guess who runs this great big machine of international trade, loot and finance? It is a 'cabal' of secretive bankers. They are low key, not in the news ... but very powerful men who control the almighty dollar."

"I saw a great documentary about these guys. More than one hundred years ago, this group of bankers and some very powerful industrialists got together to lay down a framework for running the world and moulding it to suit their needs. They wanted to bring order into what they thought was chaos. The cabal started from Europe but now includes the Americans too. They are the ones who now control the world."

"What about the big corporates? Don't they play a role too?"

"Of course, they do ... but the big boys are the bankers. They finance the cartels. It is a neat arrangement. And if any person or group of people or country is perceived as a threat to this order, the reprisal is swift and overwhelming."

Kundan paused and then added passionately:

"Look what they did to Iraq. They destroyed a land with a lie. Hundreds of thousands dead ... millions of refugees. For more than fifty years they have been strangling Cuba. The world knows it's wrong. They are screwing Iran and Venezuela. Look how Israel does what it pleases and gets away with it. The United Nations knows it's wrong. Does it matter? They control the resources of Latin America and the continent of Africa and everyone knows they have the world by the balls and they can't do a damn thing."

"Do you think you and I matter? Do you think all those millions of people protesting about wars, injustice, rising prices, bad health care and education, affordable housing, police brutality, really matter? They don't, but they are making a difference, and this is what the cabal fears the most. Ordinary people and their growing angry voices ... how do you shut them out?"

Kundan's voice dropped to a dramatic whisper:

"To do that, they have to control the information the world receives. This is critical. It is a mind game. Most of the avenues of mass media are under their control ... and to keep us from thinking more deeply, every single raw fucking emotion will be used to divide, emasculate all of us: patriotism, entertainment, sports, fear, hysteria, nationalism, race, religion ... to prevent any rational discourse that sees the larger picture. Their motto is simple: 'If you have to think, don't think beyond your nose. Live in your little island, amuse yourself ... we will run the world for you.'"

Then he smiled and said,

"I've made quite a speech, haven't I?"

I believe he had. But more than the speech, I had never seen a night sky viewed this way. Only Kundan could do it. Secretive men in dark shadows with deep pockets and vile intentions running our world ... and stopping people from thinking too much.

Did it matter if this theory was true?

What I did know was that both poor people and poor countries had lost control over their destinies. The world's economic and political system was so heavily skewed in favour of the powerful, particularly those who controlled vital resources and finance, that the rest of the planet was automatically disenfranchised. It would be damned difficult to break free and be accepted at the high table as an equal.

And as far as controlling the news and information was concerned, it was no longer a secret that most of the international mainstream sources had 'agendas' that pandered to the needs of the same economic and political system, and there was no such thing as a free and independent media. News was either biased or just plain fake. Genuine information about the state of world affairs would have to be rigorously sought out ... discovered ... or painfully sifted from the dungheap of misinformation. Or gathered from alternative sources and from people who had the fortitude and courage to stand up and speak out.

But a question needs to be asked ...

How had Kundan turned so radical in his thinking?

An early lesson began with Afghanistan.

It was 1985 and Kundan and I were visiting some friends of mine at the office of the Communist Party of India (Marxist) in Delhi. It was Kundan's first real contact with 'leftists', and he was a bit cautious as I introduced him to Rajen Prasad and Sitaram Yechury, both up-and-coming party functionaries.

As we lounged on the lawn of the office on Ashoka Road, a group of young people walked in. They could have, with some imagination, passed off as Indians, but we knew they were not. We found out that it was a delegation of teachers, four men and six women, from Afghanistan paying a courtesy call to fellow 'socialists' in their neighbourhood. Some were dressed in traditional attire, and some in shirts and trousers and tops and skirts.

Later, the delegation joined us on the lawn and Kundan got first-hand experience from these teachers about the events taking place in Afghanistan, because he was the one asking most of the questions.

"Why did the Soviets have to invade Afghanistan?"
"They came because the West was funding these 'mujahideen' and arming them with all kinds of sophisticated weapons."
"Couldn't the Afghan government handle this situation?"
"It could not because it was not just warlords and clerics who were fighting us.

The Saudis and others had funded thousands of fighters from the Arab world, Chechnya, Dagestan and also from Pakistan who were trained by instructors from the US. It was tough taking them on. It is easy to criticize the intervention sitting outside, but we had no choice ... we couldn't allow all the gains we had made in the last ten years to just disappear. ..."
"I still think it was wrong for the Soviets to invade."
"We invited them. When the fighting stops, they will leave."

"If you say you are doing good work, why are these people fighting you?'
"They have been told that they are fighting against people who do not believe in Allah or the Quran. Can you believe that? I am a Muslim and I believe in Allah and the Quran ... most of us do ... but we are socialists too. They have been brainwashed to believe that we are evil."

"What do you people want to achieve for your country?"
"We just want to bring change ... just like you are trying to do in India. Here you have feudalism, religions and castes. There we have feudalism, religions and tribes. It's a long journey, but we have started. We have a new Constitution that says everyone is equal ... men and women, Sunnis, Shias, everyone. No more divisions. We are all Afghans. We know it is a difficult task but we are trying."

"We have carried out land reforms and returned the land to the tiller. That has made the big landlords angry but the ordinary farmer is happy. We are building modern schools, hospitals, electricity plants, roads, factories. Change will take time ... some more time ... and these people are not making it easy."

"How do they see it?"
"They say all of this is a threat to Islam and the Afghan tradition."
"Is it?"
"How can land reforms, equality, modern education, hospitals, science and electricity be a threat to anyone? The only people who really oppose us are the tribal warlords, mercenaries and priests. Not the people ... and the western press calls these people freedom fighters, can you believe that?"

"What if they win?"

I remember that at this point a young Afghan woman intervened:
"They can't."
"Why?"
"We believe that many ordinary Afghan men are on our side because they realize that we are trying to improve their lives. We also believe that most of the women are with us and that is half the population. That is our real strength ... the women of Afghanistan. There are thousands of them working as school teachers, doctors, lawyers, factory workers, shop owners, even bus drivers! Thousands of young girls are getting a modern education. Isn't that important?"

She seemed so confident when she said it that both Kundan and I believed her.

But she was wrong.

In the end, it was 'God's soldiers' who won.

It was an early lesson for Kundan about the nature of geopolitics: about the cold war between great powers and through that, the tragic histories of both people and countries.

In 1989, the Soviet Union withdrew its forces from Afghanistan after ten years of fighting a bitter, brutal war. Within a short time, the 'socialist' government fell and the country descended into a civil war. Finally the Taliban arrived and swept aside the bickering warlords and took power. They in turn were toppled from power in 2001 by the United States and its NATO allies, who launched their 'War on Terror' and promptly put in their own version of a friendly 'elected' government in Kabul.

The Taliban retreated and another round of a savage civil war began. What Kundan did not witness was the final denouement.

The tale now.

On the 15th of August, India's Independence Day, in 2021, the Taliban entered the capital of Afghanistan, Kabul, and took over the city. The 'elected' government of President Ghani had collapsed and Ghani himself had fled the country. The Afghan army by and large had capitulated without firing a shot, and delivered a vast quantity of arms, ammunition and billions of dollars of war material into the hands of the conquerors.

With that kind of a scenario, the Americans had no room to negotiate any terms except safe passage for themselves, their allies and their families, and those Afghans who had helped them during their twenty-year occupation of the land.

Poof! they went ... just like that.

It was humiliating to witness the scenes of this shameful and hurried departure that were telecast on screens around the world. In all of this incredible and traumatic confusion the world also, for the first time, got a good look of the people who had confronted and defeated this 'invincible' war machine.

I got a good look of them too: the bearded, elderly, well-groomed leaders in their white salwar-kameezes, black jackets and turbans, holding press conferences and being endlessly interviewed by the international media. They looked reasonable, but were they? The visual memories of their previous governance were horrifying.

I also got to see their ragtag army of young fighters, some in their teens, walking on the streets of the capital or atop captured American Humvees, APCs and pickup trucks. All of them heavily armed with captured US weapons and ammunition.

Did these kids really believe that their sisters should not get a modern education, that women should not work ... and would they flog them if they did? Did they really believe that their mothers were chattel? Who had taught them this Islam?

I then asked myself other questions. Was I happy that the United States and its allies had finally left the country? The answer was, Yes. The United States was an occupying power and could never have been accepted by the majority of Afghans.

Was I happy that the Taliban had won? No. I find it extremely distasteful that religious fundamentalists should masquerade as liberators; and unfortunately, that is exactly what the Taliban have become. They have taken on that aura by defeating the Americans and other foreigners. I hope the people of Afghanistan will be given the opportunity to decide whether they are liberators or not, and I hope they choose wisely.

That also seems to be the biggest concern of the international community. They wonder if the new Taliban regime will fulfil its commitment of creating an inclusive government that will represent all factions of Afghan society and political interests, and guarantee equal rights to women and girls.

The tragedy of it all was this: more than thirty-five ago, much of what was being pleaded for now was in the process of being achieved, and it was deliberately destroyed by this very same international community. What was the net result? Years and years of war, of trying to 'civilize' a land. How many lives were lost, how much wanton destruction and how much despair, and all of this in the name of 'nation building'?

What a bloody waste! Yes, Kundan and I were witness to the beginning of this destruction.

There is also a footnote to this sordid and devastating intervention.

On one of the last days of the departures at Kabul airport, as thousands of Afghans desperately tried to flee, a suicide bomber detonated his lethal load. More than a hundred and seventy Afghans and thirteen American soldiers died. More than a hundred people were injured. The devastation was total.

The United States warned of a swift reprisal and within three days, in Kabul, a van with ten people inside was pulverized by a missile fired by a drone. The US said they were terrorists planning another attack and the White House spokeswoman said curtly:

"They had no reason to be alive on the planet."

It was a statement that seemed right out of a Hollywood film. The United States of America had responded with a dismissive quotable quote. However, the question still remained: Who were those people who had no right to be alive on the planet?

The tragic truth ...

They were not terrorists but members of two families who were preparing to go for an outing ... just an ordinary drive. They were three adults and seven children, the youngest being a girl who was just two years old. All of them vaporized into nothingness. The grieving father who was in another vehicle quietly whispered to a visiting reporter,

"I will never forgive them. Never! All they did was to bring grief to our land and people. I am glad they have left."

A thought crossed my mind: How many thousands of innocent civilians have died in similar strikes over the years? How many thousands of grieving families were left behind to mourn and to hate?

Kundan's retaliation

It must have been around 2008/09 and Kundan was incensed. He had recently read a report about a massive drone strike somewhere that had wiped out half a wedding party: men, women, children, even camels and sheep. It was indiscriminate slaughter.

"Just wiped out in a flash ... just mangled remains."

He shook his head in disbelief.

"You know, I saw a documentary on how these drones operate. The drones can be flying in the Middle East but the operators could be in a room somewhere in America, in Nebraska ... having a fucking cup of tea and joking around. Then comes the command and they zoom in to the area that has to be attacked. The target is located, then locked in and the fucking button is pressed. Then they count the seconds to go before contact. Suddenly there is a flash and the guys in the room celebrate. Everything clean, distilled ... no bodies to be seen, no bloodshed. Then the operators go back to their homes and kiss their wives and children goodnight and go to sleep. If they have made a mistake they have no idea of the havoc they have created."

He continued:

"Sometimes I wish some these drone missiles get their coordinates confused and strike back right up the asses of those operators."

I smiled.

"That would be an act of terror."

"Yeah, I know ... but what an idea. Just imagine it. Those smug guys sitting in that secret room with all those fancy gadgets, drinking coffee, joking and the countdown begins. As contact point is reached, 'boom', there is a flash. No more room. No more operators."

I smile at the thought of it.

Soliloquy 2

I think about those Afghan teachers
whom I had met so many years ago.
I also think about the hundreds of thousands
of Afghans who had similar dreams for their country.
They were teachers, doctors, lawyers, engineers,
workers, students, farmers, business people,
and they all believed that it was possible
to transform their land that was so divided
into a modern republic.
Was that dream really as noxious
as the western press made it out to be?
I do not think so.

Yes, there were ideological battles
between the ruling 'socialist' factions
that had seized power in Afghanistan.
It is also true that they were not elected.
But were they really, therefore, illegitimate?
Were their social and political intentions
really at odds with the wishes of most Afghans?
I do not know. Only time would tell,
and unfortunately, the time that was needed
was not given.

The West would intervene.

Anything that smelled of 'the left' was anathema.
And so, with Pakistan, Saudi Arabia
and a couple of other oil-rich countries
as flunkies and willing partners,
the US launched the project of
'GOD VERSUS ATHEISM'.
The foot soldiers of this God
were mercenaries,
war lords and rabid clerics.
And once the Soviets intervened,
it exacerbated the issue
and a 'prophecy' was fulfilled.

God won. The ways of HE/SHE/IT are mysterious.

There is however another twist in this tale.

What was hidden behind the headlines of this brutal, almost never-ending war was a secret financial and business deal that was being attempted to be struck: an incredibly lucrative natural gas pipeline from the fields in Turkmenistan that would pass through Afghanistan and into Pakistan, to the port at Gwadar. The deal was conceived by the US multinational company UNOCAL, and was worth billions upon billions of dollars.

It was a deal worth killing Afghans for.

... and kill they did.

Snippet

"It's a great series,
but I think we are going to have problems."

"Why?"

"Some of the scenes are pretty stark and brutal."

"That's why it's good."

"My friend, we are dealing with
a police station and the government of India ...
we might have some problems
with the censors. Couldn't
there be some redeeming stories?"

"The main protagonist
is an upright and honest cop ...
isn't that good enough?"

"Kundan, he's fighting a losing battle.
All the odds are stacked against him."

"That's how it is in the real world.
We researched it thoroughly ...
the good guys get shunted out.
If you heard the stories about
what really happens inside a police station,
it would make anyone sick.
I've toned it down a lot."

"You call this toning down?"

"F**k ... yes! It's actually much worse."

"Okay ... so let's hope it gets through."

Why the hell was he always on edge?

The stress-buster

The stage of taking notes and writing on a pad in dark theatres had long since passed, but what was retained was the earnestness and passion with which he approached everything ... his reading of books in the library, participating in a classroom discussion, or preparing for a project or exercise. It was intense with always the hint of a looming crisis. What was it that kept him constantly on edge? The only time I saw him relax was in his encounters with the funny man under the Wisdom Tree.

Thank god for the funny man. Thank god for the Wisdom Tree.

Let me tell you the tale of both.

As in all batches and in most educational institutions, there has to be a funny man: the wise-cracker ... the joker in the pack. In film school we had one too, and his name was Pratap Pande. Then we had the Wisdom Tree. Set in the plaza between the Main Theatre and the canteen, it was the third point of a triangle and very strategically located. It was the meeting place for debates, the telling of tales, gossip, and an open-air space for any student to express his or her opinion about any and everything. And when the students went on strike, which was often, it was space for sit-ins and speeches.

It was here that I heard Kundan Shah laugh. Whenever he and Pratap got together there would be an incredibly funny duel of seriousness and irreverence as they discussed films, theory, literature, music and just life.

Pratap was the great raconteur ... his tales about his home town Bhopal, his ideas about cinema, film theory and anything serious would have Kundan double over in laughter because Pratap had his own take about everything.

"If Eisenstein were alive, I would take him to Bhopal and teach him a thing or two about life. He takes cinema too seriously, he needs to relax. Besides, I know a lot about him, what does he know about me? Nothing!"

Then there were the dismissive announcements.

"I am following in the footsteps of Godard."
"How are you doing that?"
"He doesn't believe in writing scripts ... neither do I."
Kundan protested.
"Godard said that after making many films ... look at his body of work!"
"That's the difference between him and me. I'm saying it before I make a film."
Kundan would shake his head and laugh.

But more than just Pratap's take on cinema, it was his fascinating stories about the people of his home town, Bhopal, that would have Kundan thoroughly engaged. Erotic tales of secret love affairs, of illicit homosexuality, tall tales of hunting and heroism ... irreverent anecdotes of street corner story-tellers and gossips who mocked the high and mighty and who had no qualms about extending the truth and other colourful characters who gave this little town in the heart of the country its incredible reputation of being the tall-tales capital of India.

Yes, Pratap was Kundan's therapy: his stress buster.

One day as we sat discussing some aspects of film-making under the Wisdom Tree, our court jester joined the group with a question.

"What, my wise friends, is the basic difference between the cinema of Federico Fellini and Michelangelo Antonioni?" he asked.

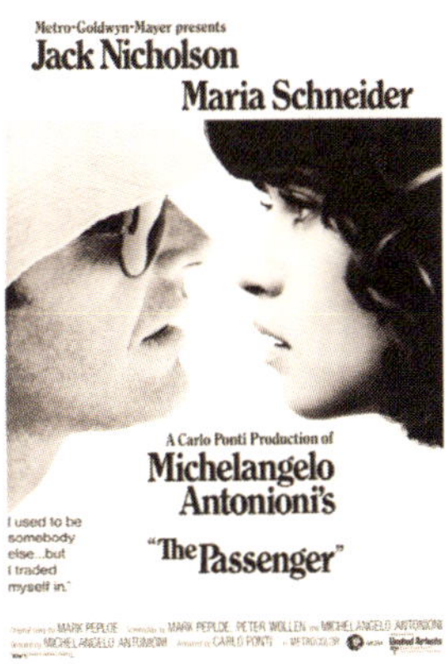

The question seemed simple enough – yet was the answer simple too? Our funny man surveyed our confusion, then laughed and provided the answer to his own question.

"Let me enlighten you people. Fellini uses his budget to fill up the frame and Antonioni uses it to empty it out!"

He laughed and stretched out his palm for the rest of the class to slap in appreciation because he knew it was a clever answer ... simplistic and, strangely enough, true. The analysis was not really deep but just the kind a wise guy would come up with. So, our funny man got his due appreciation and set us thinking.

Fellini's cinema was alive and celebratory, filled with people, objects, music. It was welcoming and opulent. It had memory and nostalgia, and, as our funny man noted, to create that kind of cinema you needed a matching budget.

Antonioni, on the other hand, saw a bleak, dehumanized world devoid of emotion ... alienated and desolate. He emptied out his world to its basic essentials, which also required an enormous budget. Two different kinds of cinema, two different world views ... and both the film-makers had emerged from a devastated Italy after the Second World War.

"He's right", muttered Kundan and smiled.

Our funny man had come to this conclusion by just closely watching the cinema of these two masters. His views will not be found in any text book, but it was a view that he had personally arrived at and it was his 'eureka' moment.

And this, precisely, is what the film school did to each and every student.

It allowed them to reflect, to make mistakes and recover from them, to arrive at conclusions and, fundamentally, discover themselves. It did not matter whether you were an editor, cinematographer, director, actor, screenplay writer or sound engineer ... when you graduated from here, you were not just seeing cinema in a different way, you were also seeing the world differently; when you left that space you were a changed person – transformed. Questions about cinema resounded in your mind: is it art ... is it entertainment ... is it personal ... is it political?

Finally, of course, there was the choice we all had to make when we graduated: Did we want to be a part of the mainstream world of cinema or did we want to change it ... or even be outside of it, in a nowhere land?

The film school was a place of magic.

It was also a space for some juvenile fun.

... and naked came Kundan.

The word spread swiftly on campus. Kundan was trapped naked in the common bathrooms of the hostel and Pratap Pande had invited everyone to witness the consequences. No, it was not ragging time and Kundan was no 'fresher'. In fact he was a respected senior, but that did not matter to our funny man.

He was a respected senior too.
So, when Kundan, as usual,
with his towel wrapped around his waist,
walked the twenty yards from his room
to the common bathrooms,
Pratap hatched his plot.
He knew Kundan would toss the towel
over the wall, shower, sing a few
tuneless songs, and then dry himself
with the towel, wrap it around his waist
and head back to his room
to change into fresh clothes.
The whole exercise would take
around fifteen minutes.

This time the funny man took the towel down
as soon as it appeared on his side of the wall
and invited the students to witness
the drama that would follow.
Quite a few students took up the offer.
They lined the corridor
that led from his room to the baths and waited in anticipation.

They were let down. There was no drama.

Kundan finished his bath and the waiting students knew it.
There was about a minute's silence and then Kundan emerged wearing nothing but his glasses and casually sauntered past the students. He entered his room and shut the door behind him and then yelled,

"This is nothing you bastards ... learn to bare your souls!"

There was one man who helped Kundan do just that.

The Man

We were in the middle of our second year when the great man visited us. Ritwik Ghatak. He was a legend with the students at film school and even though he did not have a large body of work, he was revered for his iconoclastic style and, most importantly, for the palpable passion behind his cinema.

As luck would have it, he agreed to take a class with our batch.
The session started and the students began to ask him questions on his use of music ... the kind of camera lenses he found most conducive for his work ... anecdotes on the handling of actors ... the need for silence.

As we were discussing all of this, Kundan raised his hand. I was surprised. Ritwik-da was in his element and holding forth eloquently, and suddenly there was this interruption. I looked at Kundan slightly annoyed. Ritwik-da looked at him inquiringly ...

"Yes, young man ...why have you raised your hand?"
"I have a question, sir."
"What is it?"
Kundan looked a bit embarrassed, then asked:
"How does one become a good director?"

I was surprised. What kind of question was that? It seemed so childish. Just when we were getting started on a great conversation and discussion, did we have to have this? Yet, when I looked at Kundan again I knew he was serious ... desperately seeking answers. Perhaps Ritwik-da noticed that too. He thought for a while and then answered.

"Read the text books on cinema that you need to read. Learn everything you need to know about technique. But a good director retains his childhood in one pocket and keeps a bottle of alcohol in the other."

There was silence for a while as we all decoded that statement in our own ways. Ritwik-da looked at Kundan and asked,
"Have you got your answer, young man?"
Kundan nodded slowly...
"Yes, sir."
"Can you reveal it to us?"
"Trust yourself. Back your intuition."

... and Kundan did just that.

Snippet

"What's wrong with a 15-page monologue?"

"Does it have to be that long ... can't it be shortened?"

"It's a discourse on life ..."

"I know, I know ... but that long?"

"When you are dealing with the suicide
of three young women,
the meaning of life matters.
Try and imagine
what those young girls went through.
So the audience will have to listen ...
it can't be shortened."

"Kundan, this is cinema,
not reality ... there is a difference."

"What is the difference ...?"

"Why the hell do you have to be so obstinate?
That speech is too long
and it doesn't work for me."

"Okay, okay ... I'll give it another thought."

CHAPTER 5

A Conversation with Nazir

Late evenings are wonderful on a houseboat. The sun has just about set and most of the daily activities on the lake are coming to a halt and the nightly ones just beginning: honeymooners or romantics now decide to take a leisurely ride on a *shikara* and look at the moon and stars, and late night tourists from north and west India want to sing Hindi film songs with their family and friends.

There are other Kashmiri salesmen on their *shikaras* offering *seekh kebabs*, snacks, salads and sodas to the romantics and singers and to those guests on the houseboats who are about to settle down for a drink or two or three.

It is also time for my early dinner and Nazir sahib arrives with the meal. He had been informed earlier that I avoided dinner and relied on a soup and perhaps a sandwich, both, preferably, vegetarian. But the sly Kashmiri and owner of the houseboat had an ace up his sleeve.

He prepared a stew. Not a soup but a stew with all the vegetables in the world: carrots, onions, tomatoes, potatoes, beans, cauliflower, pumpkin, spinach.
What could be more vegetarian than that? Then he added the '*coup de grace*': delectable pieces of marinated mutton and a little saffron tossed into the boiling cauldron. Along with the stew came large portions of Kashmiri bread. Yes, Nazir sahib was not going to allow a fellow 'Muslim' starve to death.
So when he saw what I had finally consumed he was shocked.

"You have barely touched the mutton in the stew", he complained.
"I loved the pieces of mutton ... and your stew was fabulous."
"It does not show with what I have left ..."
"I have eaten enough meat in my life Nazir sahib ... I need to give my stomach a rest."
"Why ...?"
"I was very ill. I have recovered ... but I have to be careful. I hope you understand."
He nodded.
"Can I ask you a question?"
"Of course."
"What is this book you are writing?"
"Oh ... just some memories of a friend ..."
"Will you be also writing about Kashmir?"
"I don't know ... maybe. Why?"
He seemed bothered.
"Is something the matter?"
"No, not really ... most journalists or writers who come here seem so friendly ... then they go back and write strange things about Kashmiris ..."
"Like what?"
"All kinds of things, sir ..."
"Do you think I will?"
"I don't, but it worries me ... worries all Kashmiris. It is difficult for you to really understand what we're going through ... what is in our hearts."
"I know that, I will never be really able to ..."
Nazir nodded and smiled.
"You don't realize how lucky you are ..."
"Why do you say that?"
"Do you think these are the conditions in which people should live ... children should be brought up ... day after day, month after month?"
He paused and then smiled.
"I'm sorry ... I speak too much. Who is this person ... the one you are writing about?"
I looked at him for a moment, then answered:
"I think he would be a friend of Kashmir."

The tale of the Kashmiri cab driver

This takes me back to late 1989 and there was a heated discussion taking place in our office on Kashmir. The militant insurgency was beginning in earnest: people were dying, young men were crossing the border into Pakistan to be trained in warfare, central military forces from Delhi were being flown in to quell the revolt, chilling Islamic slogans were being raised in the night, Kashmiri Hindus were feeling alienated and threatened and the people in our office in Mumbai had begun taking sides ...

"Why did we have to rig the elections?"
"Who says it was rigged?"
"A hell of a lot of people in Kashmir."
"It's Pakistani propaganda."
"Look at the reports in the media."
"Even if it was rigged ... did you want those fundamentalists to win?"
"Yeah ... if you heard some of their slogans ... frightening!"
"So you rig the elections? There are hundreds of thousands of angry young people now out on the streets..."
"The tragedy of it all is that it's going to give Pakistan a handle to interfere."

It was Kundan's intervention that stayed with me.

"You know, last year my family and I went on our first real holiday and we went to Kashmir: my wife, my two daughters and I. After almost ten years of slogging I thought we deserved it. We went in style. Flew to Srinagar and hired a tourist cab for the entire ten days that we were there."

"That Kashmiri cab driver made our holiday. He was the nicest human being I have met ... friendly, courteous ... and he made my daughters so happy with all those beautiful stories about the land, its history, its myths and legends.
The girls were mesmerized by those tales. It was only when he dropped us to the airport for our return that he told me very privately about the tension and anger that was brewing in towns and villages ... and that he was glad we would not be around to see it.'

"That's all I have to say."

There was silence for a while, then someone said,
"What has that got to do with what we are talking about?"

"Nothing. We are sitting here and talking about what is happening over there. He is there, in Kashmir, and I hope he will be safe. This is going to get worse ... much worse."

It was a cab driver from the past and Nazir sahib in the present ... where will it all end?

However, I must move on. There are other stories to be told ... memories to be revealed ... this mural needs many more brushstrokes to be complete.

A tale of a 'free' man

The chimes rang out and my phone screen registered the caller's name as Rahat Yusufi. I hesitated to respond because I was in a dilemma. Rahat was one of those 'ghosts' of the film school: a student who, after graduating, becomes a sort of legend with each incoming batch because of the impact his work at film school has on them. He becomes a kind of shooting star: iconoclastic and brilliant. But the narrative has a tragedy attached to it. After passing out, even as his peers and contemporaries predict a great future, the student actually disappears into oblivion. He or she becomes a memory and after some time, a mystery – and our film school had a few of them.

The reasons for oblivion could be many: ignorance of the needs of the marketplace, not showing enough respect to people in power such as producers and financiers, an overdependence on alcohol or drugs, excessive pride, or just plain bad luck. Sometimes these students would disappear into fields of education, into teaching, and sometimes with a conscious decision to just walk away from it all. Nevertheless, they left behind a legacy that others were in awe of, and Rahat was one such student.

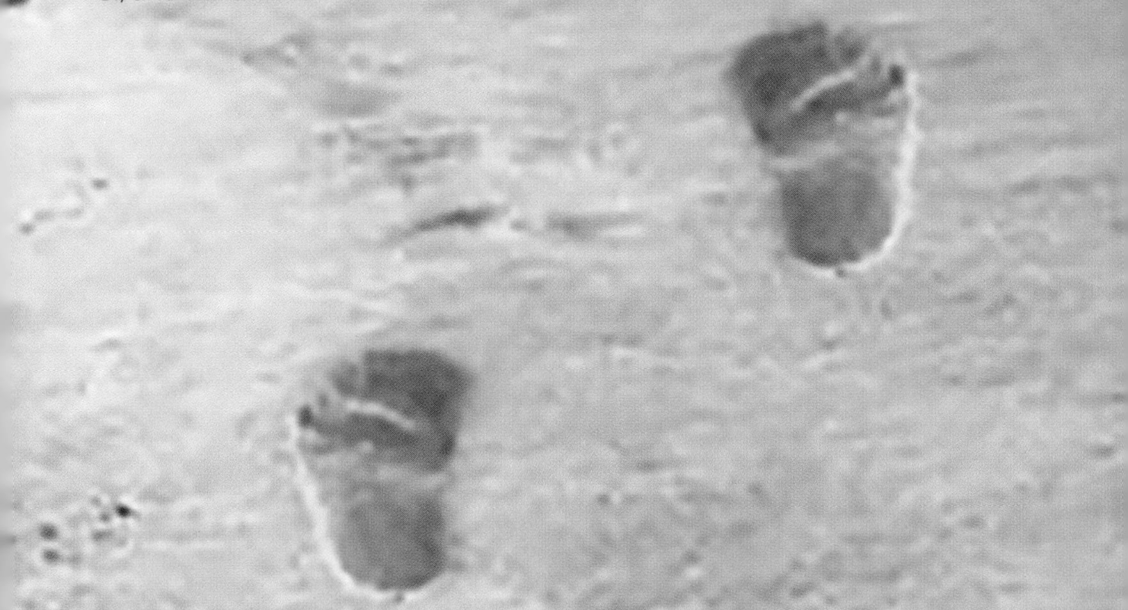

"Have you seen his diploma film?" Kundan asked.
"I have", someone replied.
"What did you think of it?"
"Good ... a bit indulgent."
"What do you mean?"
"It was good, but leading nowhere."
"What's wrong with that ... leading nowhere?"

It was clear that Kundan was an admirer.

Rahat had passed out of film school just two years before Kundan and I joined, and there were quite a few whispers about this young travelling troubadour. There were anecdotes of him quitting film jobs with great prospects. Later, there would be tales of him travelling around the northern mountain ranges meeting ascetics and scholars ... learning Sanskrit and debating with them ... learning ... this went on for years. Then there were tales of him wandering in villages in the heartland of the country and living with farmers ... tending to their fields ... searching for who knows what.

The cult of Rahat was growing.

What was it about him that struck a chord in Kundan, a deep-seated admiration? Rahat did not have a great body of work. All he had were a couple of film school projects, one diploma film that 'led nowhere', and then those numerous tales about his travels around the land.

Was that really enough? It must have been, because right through our friendship Kundan would keep reminding me of him ... of a 'free' man, in fact a wandering ascetic, with his own rules. Was that it? Was that what Kundan wanted to be?

Nine years ago, in 2012, I was to actually meet up with Rahat thanks to a piece of information I received from a friend. Rahat had been living in a small village that was not too far from my home in Goa. I decided to drive down and meet him. I found him teaching in a little village school and he lived in the home of a political activist fighting for the rights of the 'untouchables' or Dalits. Rahat looked a bit frail ... but there was a strange sparkle in his eyes, and though he greeted me warmly, I somehow felt that he did not want to be reminded of the past. His present world was completely different.

Our meeting was brief, we exchanged pleasantries, talked a little bit about (as he put it) life and destiny. Then we exchanged telephone numbers and I came away in a state of terrible sadness, thinking, was this a wasted life?

Later, a thought crossed my mind. Was he lost or was I?

And now my phone was ringing with his name on it. That name reminded me of Kundan, and also of a memory that was painful ... what could we talk about, was there really anything to talk about?

I picked up the phone ...

"Hello, Rahat."

The voice at the other end was of a man named Soumitra Chavan.

I was surprised but Soumitra explained everything to me. Rahat had had a paralytic stroke and was in a rural hospital. His right side was affected. Soumitra also told me that his activist friend and host Sonavane had died two years ago.

A sadness swept over me ... Kundan and now Rahat.

When I enquired about Soumitra's relationship with Rahat he said he was from the same village, and that he and many other young people would gather around Rahat in the evenings to hear him talk about the great big wider world. Rahat would tell them tales of history, travel and adventure. This went on for years. The kids loved these stories and discussions, and they grew to love him too.

So here was Soumitra using Rahat's phone contacts and desperately trying to get in touch with either his close friends or relatives to inform them about Rahat's condition. He had managed to get in touch with a brother in the USA, but the man said he couldn't do anything because he was so far away. Soumitra told the brother that he wasn't asking for help, that he was just informing him as that was the right thing to do. As far as taking care of Rahat was concerned, the whole village would handle it because Rahat was one of them.

Soumitra then told me that he had found my name in the list of close friends and that was why he called. I thanked him, feeling strangely guilty, and put the phone down.

I thought for a while and then contacted the alumni network of the film school ... and the word spread rapidly. Within a few hours there were hundreds of friends and admirers sending in messages about the impact his cinema had had on their work and lives. They even asked if they could be of any help. It was very heartening.

But there is a tragic end to this tale too.

I found out that Rahat died two days after that phone call. This time he had a massive heart attack. The village he had lived in for so many years conducted his funeral rites. I think he would be happy to know that so many people remembered him with so much love and affection.

I believe they remembered him because he had 'poetry in his soul'. That was what Kundan had said about Rahat's cinema.

Soliloquy 3

Poetry. It was a word that he used so often. What did he mean by it? I remember the time at film school when he was deeply moved by the voice-over in the final scene of the documentary film, *Le Jolie May* by Chris Marker.

"So long as there is sadness,
you can't be happy,
So long as there are poor,
you can't be rich,

So long as there are prisons,
you can't be free."

"Great stuff!" Kundan had said. "And you don't have to be a Marxist to feel such emotions."
It was a jibe. I still remember my quick response.
"Chris Marker is a Marxist."
Kundan smiled.
"I know, I was pulling your leg."
It was almost towards the end of our final year at film school and Kundan Shah and I were getting to know each other much better ... he was even pulling my leg.

"By the way, I discovered a great poet. Faiz Ahmed Faiz."
So, I decided to pull his leg too.
"You did? I thought he was discovered a long time ago."
"Well, I discovered him today. I was reading translations of some of his poems in the library ... very powerful. A pity he's also a Marxist."

It was my turn to smile.
"Yeah ... a pity."
"I like the way he uses metaphors to get his point across. It's a very powerful tool to convey ideas."

What Kundan would not know was that a poem of Faiz would become a kind of anthem for a very large number of people in India in the year 2019. That would be two years after Kundan passed away. The poem is called 'Hum Dekhenge'.

Hum Dekhenge

A land with no poetry

(Excerpts from an *Indian Express* article)

This houseboat on the lake is a wonderful place to think. As it gets dark, I sit on the patio, drink in hand, and remember a tale of poetry.

It is an incredible story of how a group of Muslim women, mothers and grandmothers, along with their children, in the middle of a cold December day in 2019, occupied a short stretch of road in a neighbourhood called Shaheen Bagh in the city of Delhi. They had gathered to peacefully resist what they believed to be unconstitutional citizenship laws targeting the minorities. It was to be an indefinite sit-in.

So, waving the National Flag, they sat in front of a large replica of the Preamble of the Constitution of India and portraits of freedom fighters of the past ... all heroes of a secular dream that the founding fathers had for the country. Armed with these 'icons', the women of Shaheen Bagh settled down for the struggle ahead.

Then things began to add up. Students from two nearby campuses in the city protested in solidarity with the women. The police cracked down, beating randomly, using teargas, entering university libraries for further brutality. Other campuses in the country responded to the crackdown ... there was more violence, mayhem and vandalism. More campuses erupted and Shaheen Bagh became a beacon, a call for people to come together before it was too late. It almost seemed as if the floodgates had been opened and hundreds of thousands of people started pouring in to participate in the protest, to speak out and be heard.

They were writers, poets, activists, teachers, singers, painters, musicians, actors, film-makers, and thousands of ordinary citizens who came from all parts of India to stand in solidarity with the women ... and they made Shaheen Bagh an all-out platform of resistance. They were there to fight and resist intolerance and hate, to protect the freedom of speech, equality for all, the right to dissent and all the freedoms that were promised in the Constitution.

The mood was celebratory, defiant and euphoric, and sometimes poignant, and the poem that became the anthem for these people all over the country and at huge demonstrations and marches in towns and cities around the land was written by Faiz Ahmed Faiz, the internationalist Marxist poet.

It was a poem that reminded people of the inevitable arrival of Judgement Day, 'Hum Dekhenge'.

The regime, confronted by poetry, music, songs and eloquence, realized that the only way it could respond was to get down to the basics of its supremacist and ultra-nationalist philosophy. First they tried to reduce the movement to one led by Muslim fundamentalists. When that didn't work, the mainstream media called it a meeting ground for anti-nationals and seditionists. That did not work either. Then finally:

"Shoot the bloody traitors!" shouted their stormtroopers.

Savage riots broke out in the north-eastern parts of Delhi, and as the police looked the other way, shops, homes and entire neighbourhoods were destroyed and over fifty lives were lost.

Amidst all of this Shaheen Bagh went on, but it was winding down. The effects of the Corona virus pandemic and the need for social distancing began to take its toll. It was on the 23rd of March, 2020, that these women who had created history and their remaining supporters headed to their homes. Their movement had lasted about a hundred days, and what it revealed was that even the stark brutishness of majoritarian democracy could be resisted.

Poetry was the answer to ugliness. I think Kundan would have been very proud of this 'awakening'.

The police, when clearing up this historic space, made sure that nothing remained that could remind people that once, at this place, a people came together to celebrate democracy and reclaim their republic.

A thought

Will this movement resonate in the future? I do not know, though I hope it will. I say this because Shaheen Bagh was not a just a 'muslim' movement, though it was made out to be just that by large sections of the mainstream media. What had started out as a 'muslim' reaction soon morphed into a call by hundreds of thousands of concerned citizens from across the country and from all faiths, to reverse what they considered a dangerous tide of authoritarian bigotry – and more importantly, a tide that was also threatening to undo the freedoms and rights guaranteed in the Constitution to all citizens.

On the other hand, the regime in power claimed that it reflected the will of the people.

But did it?

That was the question the people of Shaheen Bagh had posed. The answer would determine the future of our ancient land. And it seemed that most of the mainstream media had decided the outcome of this debate. They called themselves the 'mainstream' media.

Others called them:

Godi media

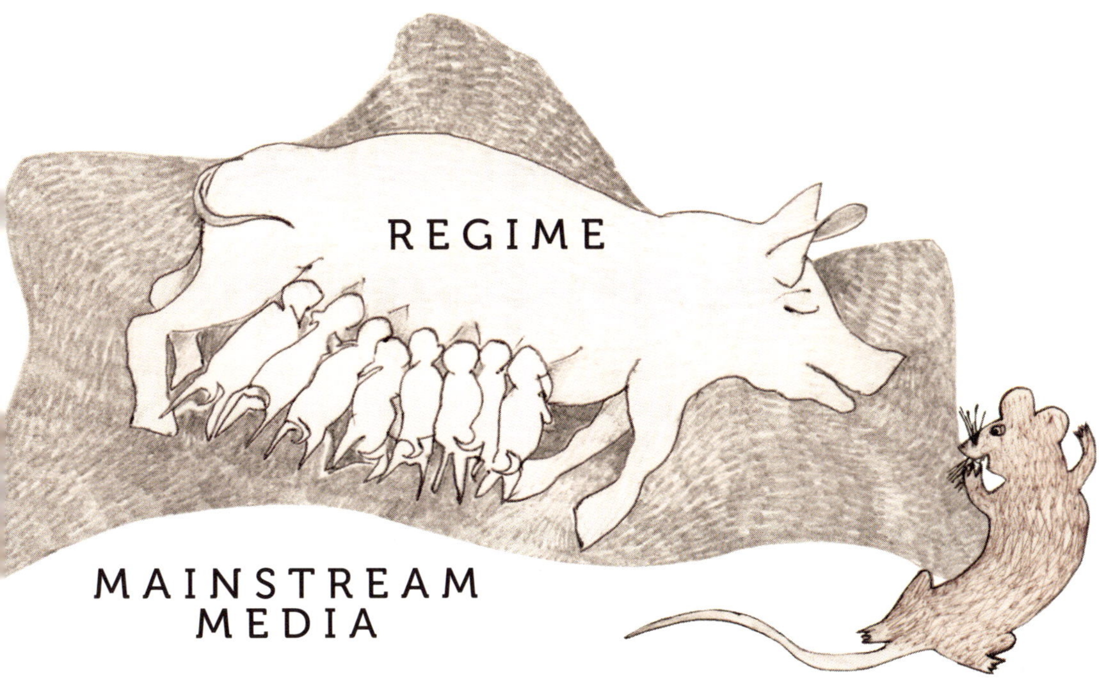

The Mainstream Media and the Sounds of Silence ... the cabal within.

If one goes by the news in the mainstream media, a great silence has descended upon my land.

The protests and agitations are over. There are no more screaming headlines about the pandemic and gruesome images of hundreds upon hundreds of deaths because of the lack of oxygen, of thousands of bodies of the poor being dumped into rivers, of others being buried in unmarked graves, and the thousands upon thousands of middle-class citizens who too have succumbed to the virus.

The deaths are only being whispered about privately and the nation has settled down to accommodate this new reality. There is very little news about the rising poverty, malnutrition, communal vigilantism and unemployment. Any act of dissent, any form of protest, has been either dismissed or relegated to the sidelines. What grabs the headlines are the foibles and fashions of cinema and sports stars, the atrocities being committed in neighbouring countries, our expanding military might and the great work being done by the regime in power.

How have the citizens responded to this state of affairs?

ONE: The rich and upper middle class, about 5 per cent of the population, have isolated themselves with each other and can always find ways to continue with their hedonistic lifestyles. In fact, they are almost relishing the fact that all their needs can be taken care of through their smart phones, television sets and other gizmos: food, fashion, electronic gadgets, medicines, children's education, payment of bills.

For entertainment too, everything is available. They have films and television programmes, porn films, documentaries, programmes for kids, channels on history and great talk shows from around the world. Then they have wonderful spiritual gurus pontificating on other-worldly issues such as Being and Nothingness. Now, discussing other-worldly issues is very important because worldly issues are screwed up and you don't really want to discuss them. In other words, these citizens have nothing to really worry about ... they can stay isolated and amuse themselves to death.

TWO: The middle class, another 25 per cent of the population, is trying to do much the same as their social superiors, but unfortunately, it is finding it more and more difficult to keep up. Times are tough and getting tougher.

THREE: As far as the rest are concerned, which means roughly 70 per cent of the population, there is a sullen anger and quiet desperation and there is no space to release it. At the bottom of this rung, roughly half, are the really poor and the marginalized. Does anyone even know what they are going through ... does anyone care to know?

Is there a conspiracy of silence, and is it planned?
Kundan would think so and so would I. Let us take a recent example.

An 84-year-old activist, who also happened to be a Jesuit priest, was branded a seditionist, arrested and sent to jail without a trial under a strange law which he could not appeal against.

He was branded an enemy of the state who, the charges said, planned to carry out terrorist acts including assassinations of certain politicians. The intelligence agencies and the police claimed they had the proof, and that they were building up the case to bring it before a court of law where he could then present his defence. In the meanwhile, they said, he was still a dangerous man, perhaps a terrorist, and needed to be incarcerated.

They were talking about a frail, 84-year-old man.

As the old man's health deteriorated drastically, he also got infected with the Covid virus. The appeals for his release within the country grew louder and international outrage brought in so much pressure that the state relented and sent him to a hospital under police custody. It was too late and after two weeks in hospital, the old man died.

Did this incarceration and death make the news in the mainstream television and print media?

It did not. Except for a very few brave newspapers and television channels, it was covered perfunctorily by most of the mainstream media houses, dismissed or relegated to the back pages. They knew that the attention span of citizens was limited and most people would soon forget.

They were right.

What grabbed the headlines at the same time of the old man's death was the cabinet reshuffle and changes that the Great Leader had orchestrated to improve his government's governance. The news was full of praise for the Great Leader's foresight in finally bringing able ministers to manage the country's teetering financial, industrial, health and social conditions, and the mainstream media became his cheer-leaders. Not one of them asked why the country was in such bad shape despite his flawless governance.

As they say in India:
they were the Band, Baaja and Baraat.

In all of this a thought remained:
why was it so important to ignore
the tragic death of the 84-year-old?

The answer was simple.

That old man was fighting for the rights of the poor and the disenfranchised. And if you covered his life and death, you would have to also cover the incarceration of many other activists who were languishing in jails under similar charges of sedition. Were they guilty or were they fighting for justice for the poor, for equality, for freedom from state brutality, freedom from hunger, for decent jobs, education and health care ... issues that are of immense concern for the vast majority of Indian citizens?

Therefore, the question arises:
What would happen
if the citizens of the country
got to know
who these people really were?
Were they then really criminals ...
terrorists?

It was on social media that
another reality was revealed...

It was a magnificent display of people's power

It was on social media that another reality was revealed. Hundreds of thousands of farmers, their wives and children hit the streets to protest against agricultural laws that the regime had rammed through Parliament without a debate. For months they had been on the streets and some estimates say it was the largest demonstration of people's power ever seen in the country ... perhaps in the world. Finally the regime caved in, and repealed those laws.

The people had broken through the walls of silence. They had to be heard because they could not be stopped ... not even by the 'cabal'.

Did you hear that, Kundan?

CHAPTER 6

The Floating Garden

It is very early in the morning and a light mist has settled on the lake in front of me. I notice an old man, perhaps my age, paddling his *shikara* across the water. It is a beautiful sight because the *shikara* is full of flowers and it looks like a moving garden. The old man notices me observing him and deftly turns his boat towards me. I want to stop him from doing so because I have no intention of buying his flowers.

Too late.

The *shikara* is right up against the houseboat and the old man smiles.

"Flowers, sir?"

I shake my head.

He says,
"Jenaab, can there be a better way to start the day?"

I smile.

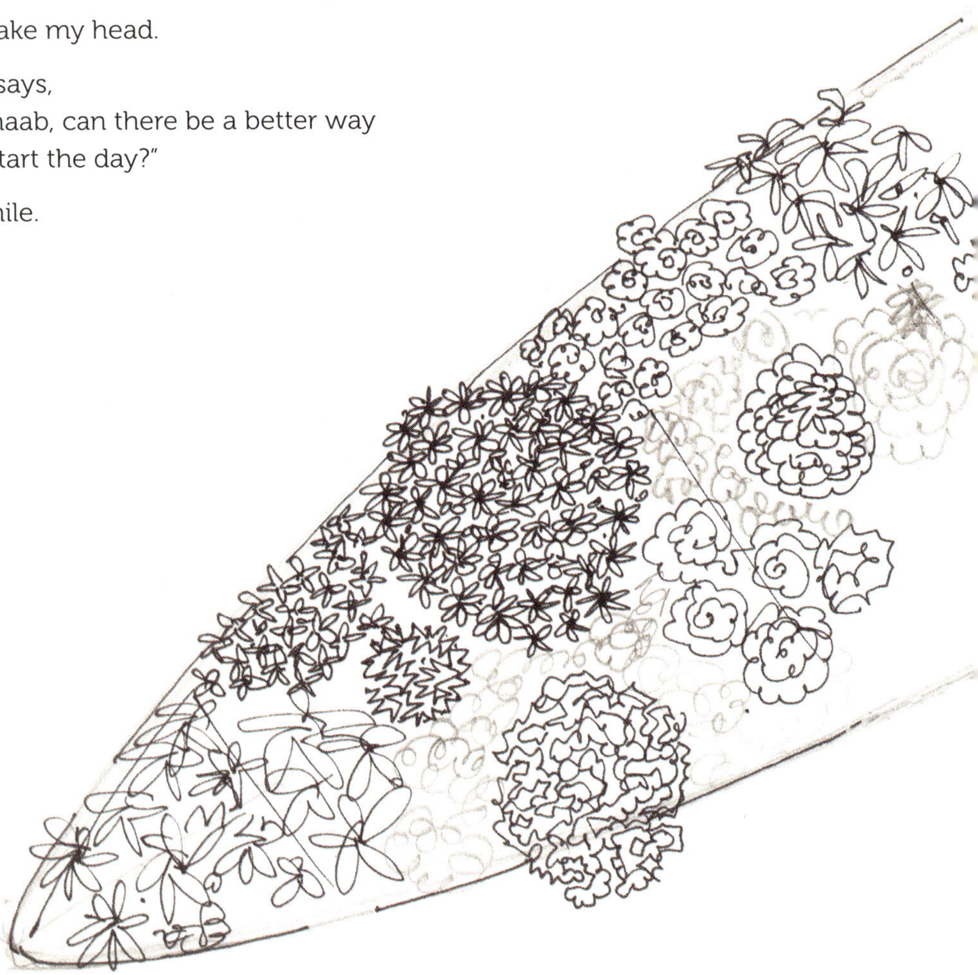

"At my age? I don't know."

"Why do we give up on beauty?
It is never too late
for anything, especially flowers."

I end up buying a bouquet.

The man smiles and paddles his *shikara*
and floating garden away.

"Khuda Hafiz."
"God be with you too", I reply.

I watch him for a long while as he paddles his
floating garden past a few house boats,
turns a corner and disappears.

It was going to be a beautiful day.

One step forward ...

The surprise party and a minor revolution.

It was their twenty-fifth wedding anniversary but since Bakula Shah did not believe in such western milestones she had planned a quiet dinner with her husband Kundan and their two grown-up and spirited daughters, Tvisha and Shilpa.

The daughters, however, had other plans for their parents, especially Tvisha, the freshly returned US graduate, with Shilpa as a willing accomplice. They would throw a special party for their parents and call a few of their closest friends.

The friends were informed about the party and told to arrive at a particular time before Bakula and Kundan returned home from their night walk, which was around 8.30 pm.

So, what was so special about this party? It was a minor revolution.

As Bakula and Kundan entered the elevator to their apartment building they were joined by three delivery men with several huge boxes of food. When Kundan asked what floor they wanted to go, they said the fifth. Bakula was surprised. It was their floor. When they asked for the apartment number, it was theirs. Kundan was surprised but Bakula was astonished. If she had not ordered anything, who had? And besides, there was a strange aroma from some of those boxes. She was sure that there had been a mistake.

There was no mistake.

When the five of them entered the apartment they found fifteen of us and two spirited daughters.

"Party time!" said Tvisha.

We had a great get-together because Tvisha had also organized the soft drinks, beer and whiskey. Bakula had a great time too with all the singing, nostalgia and camaraderie.

She had one complaint, however: Why had Tvisha also ordered those chicken dishes? Couldn't the meal have been vegetarian?

Tvisha's reply was revealing ...

She smiled and said that most people in the room were non-vegetarian and so were Kundan, Tvisha and Shilpa when they went out with friends. Then she added:

"Today is a special day. So I thought, let's break the rule of this house just once to prove we are not stuck in a groove."

I looked at Kundan. He was looking at his daughters in admiration.

... and two steps back

Was this the birth of a new nation?

On the 5th of August, 2020, the foundation stone of the Ram temple at Ayodhya was being laid and the Great Leader, after performing peripheral religious functions, finally settled down in front of the priest. Between them was a pit in which silver bricks were laid, and the priest recited the relevant Sanskrit *shlokas* for this auspicious day.

Every single television channel across India covered this function live with euphoric running commentaries as if this was the dawn of a new era.

Perhaps it was.

When seeing all of this I was reminded of the title of the D.W. Griffith film, *Birth of a Nation*. And, as with all births, there had to be a cause. Approximately nine months earlier a historic judicial 'verdict' had been delivered which happened to be the cause and this was the effect.

The baby had arrived almost on time.

A judgement and another promise fulfilled

In the year 2019, the Chief Justice of the Supreme Court of India was in a hurry to deliver justice. It seemed that both he and the government of India were tired of the delays that were taking place to decide the fate of a piece of land that had evoked such antagonistic passions that hundreds upon hundreds of people had been slaughtered because of it.

It was a space where a medieval mosque once stood and which was brought down by violent mobs who believed that it was built on the exact same spot where Lord Ram, the great Hindu god, was born. To them, therefore, the mosque was a grotesque reminder of imperial high-handedness and it had to be demolished.

So, the wise judge, and the regime in power, felt that if something was not done immediately about its ownership, this piece of land would remain a festering, cancerous wound on the soul of the republic.

About thirty years earlier Kundan Shah had felt the same way.

So let me present to you the two 'judgements' that were offered: one by a film-maker and the other by the pre-eminent member of the judiciary.

The judgement in the graveyard ...
It was late at night, towards the end of January 1993, and I was sitting in a graveyard as my city, Mumbai, was burning. It had been convulsed with horrific communal riots for more than twenty days and hundreds of lives had been lost, homes and businesses destroyed, in the aftermath of the demolition of the Babri mosque in December 1992.

I have written in an earlier book about being in the graveyard where my mother was buried and how depressed I was about the events happening around me. What I had not revealed then were the two companions who accompanied me on this impulsive and dangerous journey as the city burned and vicious and unrestrained mobs were out on the streets thirsting for more blood: They were Kundan Shah and Mukesh Sharma, a writer friend.
We were three idiots in a graveyard.

Could there be a more convenient place in times of a massacre?

It was here that Kundan tried to cheer me up."This is not really India, Saeed ... just a bunch of thugs running amok. A bunch of f*****g cowards who know that the cops won't touch them."
"That's not the issue Kundan, it's not these riots ... the issue is, where do we go from here? The mosque has been brought down, now what?'
"Simple ... it has to be built back, brick by f*****g brick ... and in f*****g slow motion ... so everyone gets the idea that a law has been broken."
I smiled.
"That is no solution. And, isn't it a bit too late to lay down the law ...?"

We got back into the car and drove to my home in silence. But our conversation did not end because Kundan accompanied me to my apartment. He had things to say.
"I know you are depressed ... so am I. But let me tell you that I meant every word I said, knowing it is too late. A country should have the balls to go against popular opinion ... because popular opinion doesn't mean that if ten guys say I'm drunk, I had better lie down."
"What you suggested was not a solution, you were saying 'up yours' to everyone ... don't you see that?"
"Of course I do ... and do you know why? I will tell you. Ever since I can remember, we never laid down the law when we really needed to. We pandered to popular perception. What happened to our Constitution?"
"Maybe our Constitution was too radical ... we are living in three time zones simultaneously ... ancient, medieval, modern."

"That's true, but that's all we have ..."
"Okay, so you accept that it's too late now?"
"I do. But, if you want to start on a fresh, clean slate, have the balls to build that mosque, brick by brick, and in slow motion. So that people can really see that a law was broken ... and has to be fixed."

I began to smile.

"Brick by brick ... in slow motion?"
"Yeah ... and I am not trying to please anybody. It was wrong, by the law of the land today, to bring that mosque down. Build it back. If I had said let's build a hospital or school on that land, there would be applause. You know why? Because it's cute. Every secularist would accept it too. So would you, because you are a Marxist and not a believer. But, my friend, most of the people in this country are ... they believe. So send a message to all believers ... you can't f**k around with the faith of others, no matter who you are!"
"That's what these guys are saying ... that the mosque was built over a temple."

"There is no proof of that."
"It doesn't matter ... people believe that ... it's a question of faith."
"Is that good enough? Besides, was there any idea of India four hundred and fifty years ago? Was there a Constitution? Don't give me that shit ..."
"Are you a believer, Kundan?"
"I am not. But don't tell my wife."

Then he added:

"You know, we had a dream about our country ... and we f**d it up. We lied to ourselves ... we never really believed in justice, we just pandered to the powerful. I know it's too late to start now ... but imagine if we could do what is right. So imagine building a mosque, brick by brick, in slow motion. Then ask the Muslims: 'What would you like to do now?' I bet most of them will say they will convert it into a hospital ... or a school ... or even build a temple alongside."**

"What if they don't?"
"Tough luck ... but don't take the easy way out."

Imagine.

That was Kundan's judgement. It was brutal. It was honest. I also know it would never be accepted as a solution. Despite the words in our Constitution that champion a secular culture, there was a vast constituency of people that had been nurtured to believe in a singular perception of the past, of glory and greatness that had been snuffed out by the 'barbaric' invasion of 'outsiders'.

I will come to this subject later.

Let us now come to the judgement of the Chief Justice of the Supreme Court of India.

He was also out to deliver justice, some say at the behest of the ruling regime, but unfortunately, he was facing charges of sexual harassment from one of his women staffers and things were looking very, very awkward. Luckily for him, the ruling regime made sure that these charges would not be an impediment to the discharge of his 'national' duties and backed the judge in every way. The case was dismissed, some say under strange circumstances, and the staffer sacked for daring to dishonour His Honour.

The ruling regime seemed to have great faith in this Chief Justice and having cleared the decks for him, withdrew into the shadows. Or so it seemed.

Then a fast-track court was set up to solve the land dispute. All previous court verdicts, all arguments and all opinions were once again placed before the Supreme Court with the Chief Justice and four other judges presiding. The proceedings were rapidly held, arguments were heard almost non-stop, and the nation held its breath.

To prove its democratic credentials, the ruling regime even magnanimously announced that it had asked all the people of the land to accept the verdict of the court, no matter what it was.

That, as Kundan Shah would say, was 'cute'. It almost seemed that the regime knew what the verdict would be because magnanimity was not one of its virtues.

Then, on the 9th of November, 2019, the Day of Judgement arrived. It was a spectacular piece of judicial jugglery and sleight of hand that would make any magician proud. It had very little to do with the law. So let me put those hundreds of pages of magical 'wisdom' in a nutshell for the benefit of readers.

In September 2019, the bench of the Supreme Court of India held that the demolition of the mosque was in violation of the law. It also held that there was also no conclusive evidence that the mosque had been built after destroying a temple, and the 'miraculous' appearance of those idols inside the mosque in 1949 were a desecration. However, the tax records showed that the land belonged to the Government of India and it should hand it over to a trust which would build a temple. This would soothe the conscience of the nation because faith had its own truth. As far as the Muslim litigants were concerned, they should be given 5 acres of land in a suitable location to build a mosque.

Simply put, the verdict was this: though the demolition was illegal, the assertion that the mosque was built after the destruction of a temple unverifiable, and the 'miraculous' appearance of those idols fake, the land was handed over to the demolition squad. Faith had its own truth.

The land was handed over
to the demolition squad.
Faith had its own truth.

Two judgements: the first very few would accept, and the second most of the nation applauded. It says a lot about us, doesn't it?

Soon after this the Chief Justice retired and even before the memory of his version of justice could fade away, he was given a seat in the Upper House of Parliament by the regime in power.

I have nothing more to say ... and as far as Kundan was concerned, he had said his piece anyway. And today I smile when I think of the 'postmodern' solution that he had given so many years ago.

I especially like the "in slow motion ... brick by f*****g brick" part. That was classic Kundan.

Yet there was something that

both of us could not comprehend.

The rising tide of hate across the country seemed inexplicable to us. By 2014 it had reached a point where almost 40 per cent of the people believed in this ideology. What and who were the forces that were driving this surge? Was it just manufactured or did it have a semblance of truth that was hidden from both of us? And, another question kept crossing my mind: what had seven hundred years of Persian, Afghan and Turkic influence really done to the existing power structures that had defined this land before the coming of Islam? Would the answer to this question explain some parts of this riddle?

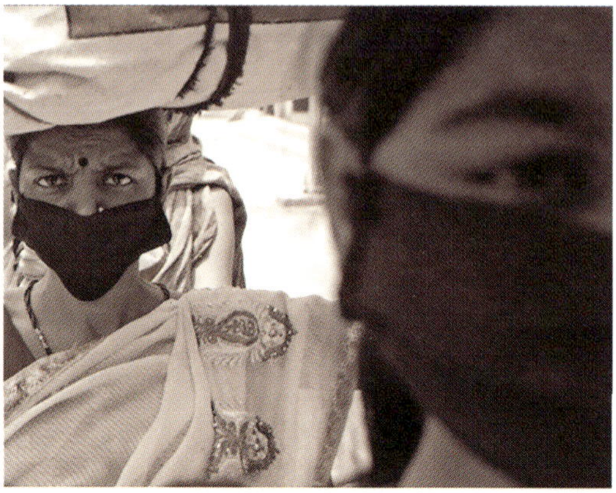

How would you define a civilized country?

Snippet

"How would you define a civilized country?"

"Tough question ... I think you judge it by
how it treats its most vulnerable citizens."

"You mean its minorities?"

"Perhaps. In South Africa the whites were the minority
but they had the power and they created apartheid ...
so it's not just minorities. I am talking about its weakest links ...
the powerless, the disenfranchised. Why do you ask?"

"I was thinking about
that vegetable vendor in Tunisia ... he was
tired of the police harassment, of the corruption ... so
he committed suicide in front of the police station
and the entire country erupted. Can you believe
that? One man's death ignited an entire country.
I call that a civilized response ... empathy ... for that man,
recognizing his pain. That is what is needed here."

"It won't happen."

"Why?"

"I think the first step is to recognize
that there is a problem. With the kind
of ruling elite we have, the middle and
upper-middle class ... basically
upper castes ... are they really affected?
Are they? Can you imagine them
coming out on to the streets to fight for justice
for the poor? Do the poor exist for them?
Do they really give a damn?"

"That is true ... they don't ..."

CHAPTER 7

The Storm on the Campus

It was towards the end of June 1975 that the storm hit the country and the film school. The central government had declared a state of Emergency.

Enough has been written about the great civil unrest that led to the clamping down, the atrocities that were committed during those years, the civil rights that were curtailed, the dissent that was crushed, the mass arrests and the many incidents of torture, and the strict censorship over the media.

For me, there also happened to be a personal angle: my sister-in-law, an absolutely delightful and energetic western classical music teacher, was picked up and branded a 'naxalite'. I could not believe it. Naxalism was a term for a militant insurgency that had taken root among the poor and indigenous people and had spread considerably in the heartland of the country. And this delightful music teacher, a member of the teachers' union who had protested against the nation-wide clampdown, was branded a dreaded militant.

It was bizarre.

How the intelligence agencies justified this charge is a convoluted story of conjecture and muddled information, but my sister-in-law spent sixteen months in jail as a political prisoner. She was incarcerated in the city of Pune in a jail that had a long history to it: many of the important freedom fighters for India's independence had also been incarcerated there. What had she done to deserve this? An extremely generous and friendly woman, open to ideas from across the world, shoved into jail, leaving her husband and three children in a state of shock. Where were the institutions that were supposed to protect human rights? Where the hell was the law of the land? How could ordinary citizens appeal for some kind of justice?

Late at night, as I sat with friends in my room at the hostel on campus, there was a knock on the door. It was Kundan. I was surprised to see him.

"I just came to tell you, I am on your side. We cannot be silent in times of tyranny."

He turned and left. Kundan had just taken a political stand.

Luckily for the film school, we had a director who did not bow to the diktat of the state and allowed the students to express themselves. His name was Girish Karnad and he made sure that the campus remained a space for free speech; and to prove it, we had special screenings of underground and revolutionary films from around the world.

The impact this had on the students was enormous. Two films come to mind. The first was *Hour of the Furnaces*: a gritty, powerful exposé of the military coup that took place in Argentina. The film covered the violence unleashed by the military junta and the various forms of resistance of ordinary citizens. The students in the audience were stunned by the film's raw power.

The second was a film that covered the revolt of the Algerian people against French colonial rule, called *Battle of Algiers*. For the first time the students saw a film in which real people, not actors, were involved in documenting their own history and their own battles for freedom and independence. The film was absolutely magnificent and when it ended with thousands upon thousands of real Algerians celebrating their victory on the streets of their capital, the students in the auditorium stood up in ovation.

They had experienced the political power of cinema.

But the Emergency did cast a fairly long shadow on campus. A kind of silence descended everywhere, and if any political discussions took place, they were conducted in the hostel rooms and not out in the open. I know there were quite a few such discussions taking place and quite a bit of it in my room.

Once in a while there would be a wisecrack about a political leader under the Wisdom Tree, and the students would smile and keep their amusement low key so as to not draw too much attention. We were aware that there were a few informers around. Some students would add subtle political jibes in their project exercises, and someone hung the national flag upside down on the door of the Main Theatre. It was quickly pulled down.

There was, however, one act of open revolt. A final-year student decided to make his diploma film into an open allegory about the state of affairs. He called his film *Slaughterhouse 1*. It was a dark and powerful metaphor, and when it was screened in the auditorium it got a standing ovation.

There was a backlash. The film would have no more screenings. But the Director made sure that we did have at least one.

It was in this kind of milieu that the students went about working on their projects. We were now in our final year and just about finishing a project called 'Dialogue Exercise'. The students called it the 'semi-final'.

We had spent a little more than two years at film school and had done a series of projects and exercises. After each one there was a prescribed interactive session where we would discuss our work and every student had the right to critique the work of another. In the early years I still remember Kundan taking down notes on the comments made about his work. Nobody else did. They just listened. And Abbas Shaban, the exchange student from Afghanistan, would just smile and bow and say 'thank you' to every student who had a comment to make about his work. Once he even opened a bag of pistachios and passed it around.

What made Kundan different from all of us was his approach to every project. It was so apparent that he had worked meticulously on the subject, discussed it in depth with his crew, and on the day of the shoot, he had every single shot noted down on sheets of paper that he just had to complete. More often than not the shots would be too many for the prescribed time, which meant almost no breaks for tea or a smoke for a tired crew member, and at the end of the day there would be a minor crisis of unfinished business.

As usual, the funny man of our class had something to say about this.

"Kundan needs that extra time because he doesn't just shoot for his film, he shoots for our films too."

But now all of that was in the past. It was Emergency time. The wisecracks were over. We had just completed our 'Dialogue Exercise' and this time we screened the films in the auditorium and after each film the discussion was held there too. The screening of my film followed the same pattern, but I noticed that Kundan didn't say a word during the discussion that followed.

I wondered why.

Late at night there was a knock on my room door and when I opened it I was surprised to see Kundan.

"I want to talk about your work."

He came in and sat down. I was puzzled.

"Why not at the discussion?"

"I could not ... it would have sounded very rude."

I smiled.

"Okay, you can dish out your critique now."

Kundan nodded. It seemed like he was looking for the words to express himself.

"When I saw your first film, 'the continuity exercise', I liked it immensely. It gave me a great complex and I really studied hard to catch up. But I want to tell you that it was the only piece of your work that I liked. After that, all your exercises have been disasters ... at least for me ... and I thought you were wasting your time on politics rather than concentrating on your projects. This time your 'Dialogue Exercise' was very good. You know, I always felt that you people lack a sense of poetry ... but this film has it. It has given me a complex and once again I feel I need to catch up."

"Catch up with what?"

"Just catch up. I have to find that confidence too ..."

I tried to understand what he had just said.

"Thanks for the praise ..."

Kundan got up and left. I wondered what he had meant by 'confidence'. Years later I would find out.

For the next six months our batch worked furiously on the final diploma project, and as directors we did not have a lot of time to spend with each other.
A casual discussion here and there about a script was about all that we could do. The planning was hectic and each one of us put everything into it. All that we had learned over the last two-and-a-half years would now come into play.
As our funny man put it,

"We will all be exposed!"

And then it was all over.

Our final films were ready and the entire batch sat down to see the films one by one as they emerged from the laboratory. Towards the end we got to see Kundan's film.

I did not have a clue about his script idea but I did remember one scene being shot in which there was a frenzy of outdoor activity. It seemed a bank was being robbed by a gang of thugs and there were a great number of bullets being fired with no one dying. I wondered what the film was about.

It was a gem. A piece of controlled anarchy at the end in which three members of the gang simulated suicide by blowing their brains out and two walked into the distance on a lonely stretch of road calling out to no one in particular. They were walking to nowhere.

As the film ended there was silence in the auditorium for a few moments. Then a spontaneous applause erupted all around and Kundan raised his hand in acknowledgment. The shouts and whistles resounded for quite a long time.

"What a piece of work!" – I thought to myself. I was glad that over the past six months we had become friends.

Our three years were over and the entire batch shook hands, hugged each other and headed out to different destinations: some to the north, some to the south, and some to the east. The exchange students headed back to their home countries.

I settled down in Bombay (it was still Bombay then) and began working on my first feature film project with a group of close friends from film school. I heard that Kundan and the 'gang of three' had moved to the city of Hyderabad in the south. Perhaps they found this monster city of dreams and disasters too intimidating.

As we worked on my script and finalized production plans I heard that the 'gang' was doing some small projects: low-budget advertising films for the city's traffic police, for local municipalities, and for some small retail outlets that did not have the budget to engage the services of the big advertising agencies. We also heard that they were finding the going tough in Hyderabad and were just about making ends meet.

Then I got busy with the shoot of my film and all the post-production details that followed. In about six months time I completed my first feature film and I was elated. That was when I heard another piece of news: Kundan had gotten married and had migrated to England with his bride. He had quit film-making.

What?!

I was stunned and I thought to myself, "What a waste ... what a waste!"

Testimonial: Pankaj Purandare, ex-student of the film school

My first impression of him was that he was a humanist – wanting to be with people, talk to them and tell them what he thinks about the world around him. He would grab you by the neck and say it – whether you were a first-time entrant in his office or a lifelong friend, it did not matter ... his energy was infectious.

I still remember the first day in his office after I joined him and he asked me why I wasn't writing. I said I'd go home and write. He said,

"You will never go home and write. You have to write here."

I tried to dodge the issue and said I was not carrying a pen or paper. He pointed to an old iron Steelman cupboard in his office and said:

"In that are my old rejected scripts. Write on the backs of those cyclostyled typed sheets!"

I was shocked.

Which film-maker would have the guts to say that about his scripts? To reveal the fact that they had been rejected ...? He could have said anything else.

He had two dozen pens of two rupees each. He'd point out and say,

"Take a pen and write. When it's over, take another. But remember, not before the first one is over."

I used to laugh about this ... the man wanted nothing wasted. Including rejected scripts.

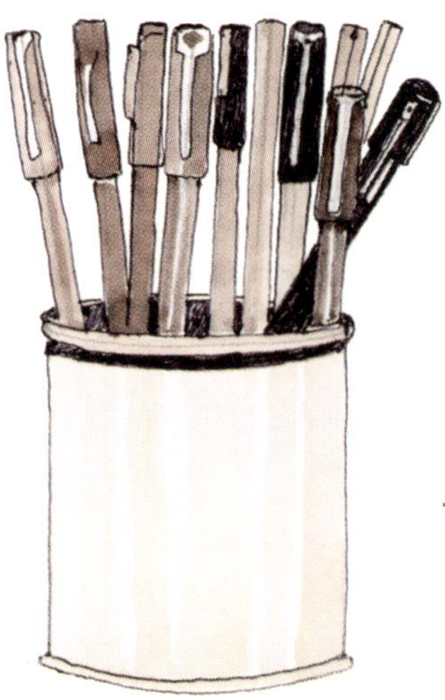

There were times when people would ask me what Kundan Shah looked like. What could I say?

"He used to be in a terrycot shirt and trousers ... the really off-the-shelf kind ... so that he perhaps looked like an insurance agent or a guy in a government office ... not the manager, not the boss, some mid-level functionary ... but he definitely didn't look like a film director."

Perhaps he found 'trying to look like one' a waste of time.

Another interesting thing was that after 6.30 pm, the pens were to be put down and the office would shut down. Just like a regular office. At 10 am, the 'office' would open. Then he'd go for lunch and he would ask us to eat within a given budget from a restaurant down the road. We would have lunch and return and he would check the accounts carefully. Then we would start writing again at 2.30 pm, and at 6.30 pm work would stop.

In the beginning, every pore in me rebelled at the idea of writing from 10 am to 6 pm. We were supposed to be the creative type, not machines. We needed time to think ... relax. Not with Kundan.

"Think at home ... here, you just write!"

Every day the first one hour would be spent in discussion about what and how to write. He'd sit on his old PC and start typing. He told me he had learnt typing and his speed was 120 words per minute. A Hindi keyboard hung from the wall and he explained ...

"I type in Hindi too."

When I asked him why he learned to type, he said it was his back-up in case he could not find another job. I could not believe that answer, and at that moment I felt that this man can't be the 'famous' Kundan Shah. How could he so calmly reveal that he could have been a typist in an accounting firm or in an office.

Then I remembered all the stories about Kundan Shah I had heard when I was a student at film school: stories from Anurag Kashyap, Pankaj Advani, Sudhir Mishra and many others. The tales were hilarious and the ones about his keeping of accounts, especially so. We heard about how he would want an account of the money spent on food down to the last rupee. He would scan the bill intently and check the balance.

"The difference is just two rupees, Kundan ..."

"It doesn't matter ... the accounts have to be accurate."

"Can I pay for the shortfall?"

"No, you can't. But the next time, there should be no shortfall."

Can you believe that? Two rupees! And he said that with absolutely no embarrassment. The whiskey that was drunk in his office was the cheapest possible ... again with no embarrassment. If you came to his office and wanted a drink, that was what you would get. Even we assistants entertained with better whiskey at home. He would order *sevpuri* as post-work snacks from a streetside *bhel-wala* near the office: three *puris* for everyone, not one more. I was told that his new apartment on Mount Mary Hill was worth a fortune and here he was, taking a rickshaw to work ... and it did not seem to matter to him.

It was at this point that I intervened and asked Pankaj:

"I want to ask you a question. Do you think Kundan Shah could have said, **'I know the psychology of rats'**?"

Pankaj thought it over and then said:

"It's absolutely possible that he could have said that. In fact, he is among the few people in the universe who could have said that ... perhaps Kafka, or Dostoevsky. He loved Dostoevsky. While working for him, he asked us to read *Crime and Punishment* and *The Idiot* again."

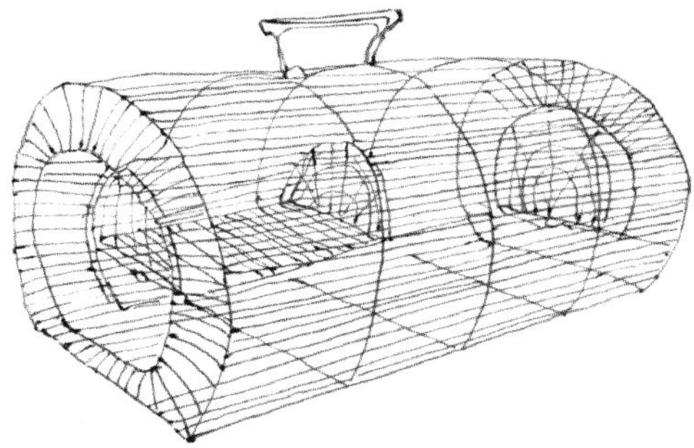

"Why do you say he was among the few who could have said that?"

"He was a conspiracy theorist and a huge one. During those days of working with him, I came to know that there were subaltern channels on the internet across the world, which he had figured out. In their news reports, when they talked about certain things, those would happen six months later. It was scary ... like predicting a future through political, economic and social analysis. Kundan recommended them to me."

"These subaltern channels are liberal. They read patterns, analysed political and financial situations, the deep inner workings of market conditions that affect global events and change history. Kundan was an aficionado and followed them."

"It was like he was getting into the whole machine, into its intestines, and seeing how it works."

"Then he came across a blue book, some kind of a CIA or Area 51 document. He made me look at these things too. When I began searching for it, I found it was banned ... there were too many firewalls."

"He had this intuitive belief that there's something happening somewhere ... perhaps he was a believer in chaos theory. A butterfly is fluttering, so a storm is brewing ... that kind of stuff. Even I have started looking for patterns."

"What also amazed me was that he wrote every single day. I wondered why."

"There were two cupboards full of rejected scripts, yet he found the motivation to write every day ... how did he manage that? When I posed the question to him, he answered with a simplicity that scared me."

"I cannot sleep at night if I have not written during the day. I need to smile and enjoy what I have written. Only then can I sleep. Sometimes I feel happy at what I have written, believing it to be a masterpiece, and sometimes I reflect on the stupidity of my work."

"Both ways I can go to sleep."

CHAPTER 8

The Return of the 'Native'

I have to take a little time over this.

I know it is no longer a secret that Kundan Shah did return to India. And yet you will have to bear with me because when he actually did, I had absolutely no idea that he would do so.

I was sitting at home with my entire technical crew planning out the script and production details of my next film. We had a month to go before we began shooting and I was getting a bit nervous. Would we be ready? It was at that point that my doorbell rang and Kundan arrived.

I could not believe it.

You should have seen the spontaneous celebration that occurred when he entered my home. All of us, ex-students of the film school, greeted him with a ten-minute interlude of hugs, backslaps, laughter, nostalgia and camaraderie, while the rest of the crew wondered what the fuss was all about. Amidst all of that Kundan turned to me and asked,

"Can you give me a job, Saeed?"

It was a simple question but when I looked at him, I knew he was waiting for an answer.
"Of course, Kundan. We've been talking about you for about two years and wondering where the hell you had gone."
"So I have a job?"
"Yes, you do. Right now."
Renu Saluja, the editor and a batch-mate, smiled:
"You can take my job too."
There was laughter all around and Kundan smiled.
"Thanks ... I'll take the first. I know it's a low budget film. I will accept whatever you will offer. But I need to know how much I will be paid."

There was an awkward silence. In a room with around twelve people it was strange to be discussing this out in the open, but Kundan had given me no choice. So I answered:
"About five thousand a month for four months ... travel and food extra."

Kundan hesitated for a moment and asked,
"Can I have my first payment in advance ... in cash?"

I looked at him and realized he was serious. He needed the money and he didn't mind saying this in front of everyone. I was stumped. I had no cash lying around.

"Done", said Saini the cameraman, coming to the rescue.
He opened his purse and took out 2,500 rupees in 100-rupee notes.
"*Saale* ... this is the first instalment. The rest you will get tomorrow ... right, Saeed?"

I nodded. Kundan took the instalment and quietly murmured,
"Thanks, Saini. I really appreciate this."
But I was surprised and asked Saini,
"Where the hell did you get that money?"
"It was a loan that I had given a friend and I just got repaid."

And that's how Kundan got his first job on his return, and I got a first-rate assistant director.

That first meeting

It was euphoric, yet heart-breaking. Yes, Kundan had returned and all of us were happy, but there was a certain sadness too. We had sensed a quiet desperation in him and though no one spoke about it, every member of the crew went about making him feel welcome and at home.

It worked.

Within a few days Kundan had snapped out of his gloom and was back at work with a vengeance. On the first day of the shoot, the *mahurat* day, we all got to meet his wife Bakula and his three-year-old daughter Tvisha.

That was the beginning.

After that Kundan was everywhere. On the sets he organized the shots, briefed the other assistant director, kept a close watch over production costs and worked through half the night on the next day's schedule. This was his work pattern every day of the 40-day shoot, and he made sure that I didn't slacken. When the shooting was over I could take just a two-day break before getting down to the editing because Kundan had organized the timeline that way.

"Saeed, a low-budget film means complete control over time. You mess up here, you run out of money. Relax after the film is ready ... not now. Don't lose the momentum."
I was amazed. The man was so bloody organized. But he had a complaint:
"Why don't you shoot a scene from several angles?"

"I don't need to. When I am satisfied with a shot, why take another?"
"It gives you an alternative on the editing table."
"I don't need it."
Kundan nodded.
"Yeah ... I noticed that. You make films very differently."

But I knew he disagreed.

Kundan sat right through the editing and all the way to the final print. The man was relentless and untiring ... and indispensable. He was about to move to another assignment, another low-budget film, but before he left I invited him home for a quiet drink. It would the first of many, many meetings.

Besides, I wanted to know more about his stay in England. I knew there was a story there.

Coming in from the cold

It was after the second drink that he began to open up.

"You know, Saeed, I haven't really thanked you for this job ... I am really grateful."
"Don't thank me, Kundan. Thank your diploma film ... that set me thinking about you."
He smiled.
"Did you like it?"
"Very much ... I think it was the best film of our class."
"Then all I can say is that it saved me."
"From what?"

He thought for a moment, and then it all came out.

"I was desperate ... really bloody miserable in England. I was in a shitty job and nothing seemed to be working out. I finally told Bakula, let's get back to India. I hear Saeed is starting a feature film and I am sure he will help me out. She was hesitant ... she didn't want to take chances ... there was Tvisha. Finally she agreed. So when I got back from your house with that cash, she finally relaxed ... and these last four months, I feel so much better."

"Tell me about England ... what happened there?"

"When we arrived we rented an apartment in Southall. It was really small – two small rooms that included a kitchen and a bathroom, and in that space were my parents, a brother, and Bakula, Tvisha and I. The Gujarati landlord knew we were desperate and he really squeezed us. Son-of-a-bitch ... all that talk of Gujarati brotherhood ... f*****g *bakwas*!"

"But what really got us was the bitter cold ... for four or five months a year it was unbearable. There was a window that had a tiny crack and through that the cold would come in ... like a knife. We could only afford heating for a few hours at night. The rest of the day and night it was freezing. We just made sure that Tvisha was well wrapped and kept warm. God, I will never forget that cold ... how I cursed it."

"Did you find work?"

"I applied for a job at the BBC and presented my film school diploma. A guy interviewed me and said he would call back and let me know. I waited for two days and then I went back. He said there might be an opening as a trainee. He would call me if it worked out. I waited for some days and then called him again. He said I would have to wait. I waited and then called again. The bastard said that I seemed to be impatient. Then he slammed down the phone."

"What could I tell him? Of course I was impatient. I was f*****g desperate. I didn't know what to do. I did a crash course in typing and luckily I got an offer of a job as a clerk in an accounting firm. I took the job, no questions asked. It was a job sending and receiving letters of credit. For two-and-a-half years, on slave wages, sending letters of credit or receiving them."

"One thing you need to know about these *desi* networks. They pay you just enough so you don't starve to death. You are expected to quit, take a loan and start your own firm, where you do the same thing to the newer entrants. What a racket!'

"I was living like a hermit in that cold land and the only friend I really had was Dostoevsky. His books kept me company.'

Then he smiled and added,

"And once in a while I used to read some 'leftist' literature."
"What?"
"I knew you would react this way."
"Did you find it interesting?"
"You know, when you are outside your familiar surroundings the philosophy of the left begins to make sense."
"What do you mean?"

"You begin to understand the psychology of immigrants ... racial tensions and hate ... and fear ... a lot of things that you would not otherwise think about. It opens up your mind, about history, economics ... politics. I spent my weekends in bookshops.'

"So, have you forgiven the left?"
He smiled.
"Yeah. ... Can I tell you a secret?"
I nodded.
"I picked up a few books that I didn't pay for."
"What?"
"I was broke but I wanted those books ... don't look at me like that ... I was broke, and hadn't the British looted us? So I did a bit of recovery."
"You ass, you could have been arrested ... how often did you do that recovery?"
"Twice."
I shook my head.
"You are a really small-time crook. If you had to do a bit of thievery, you should have had a go at the British Museum ... there is a lot of big-time loot there."
Kundan smiled, then asked:

"Any news of Rahat Yusufi?"
I was a bit surprised by the sudden question.
"No, not really ..."
"I used to think of him often in England. I wonder where he is."
"He's probably in the hills somewhere ... are you glad to be back?"
"I am. There is one good thing that I need to tell you about my stay in England."
"What is that?"
"Southall has gangs ... Indian and Pakistani gangs. When things get rough, they get together to take on the British goons. That's about the only good thing I can tell you about my stay there."
He paused and continued.
"It feels good to be back. After almost four long years I feel I am worth something. And working with you guys really has helped me a lot. I am even working on an idea for a film."
"You are? That's great news Kundan ... great news."

A thought

As I recall that conversation of so many years ago, a thought crosses my mind. In the 1970s, a move to England, or the USA, was the dream of almost every small-time businessman or trader from India. And if you were a Gujarati, even more so. There were hundreds of cases, thousands perhaps, of illegal entries, of manufactured documents or just plain 'Indian wizardry' of circumventing laws that brought these people to distant shores.

Was Kundan's family one such case? I am sure it was. The move to England was a dream ... the beginning of a struggle that would eventually lead to paradise in the future. This is the story of the millions of Indians who live there ... a gradual journey of struggle to eventually reach financial bliss. And often, this dream works.

But.

Kundan was no longer a trader ... he had tasted poetry ... and that was his Achilles' heel. He had to come back.

CHAPTER 9

The Celebration

Kundan's first film was a grand undertaking.

As soon as word spread that he was planning a film, a large number of his batchmates, some with and some without his permission, announced their intentions of getting involved: some, including me, as advisors, as writers, as assistant directors, and in the camera, editing and sound engineering departments. A group of graduates from the National School of Drama and a couple of freelancers joined the creative process too.

Kundan was the pivot, and within two months of intense writing, bickering and debates, a script was finally ready and presented to the National Film Development Corporation for approval. Kundan went ahead with his casting and production plans.

Then they got the good/bad news.

The script was approved in principle but needed to be improved with the help of a 'script advisor'. This was absolutely critical. A copy had been sent to the 'advisor' and Kundan would have to meet him. There was a small celebration as Kundan headed to the Corporation office to find out the details of this development. He returned two hours later and informed us that the meeting was fixed for 11 am the next day.

"Who is the advisor?"
"I am not supposed to reveal the name."

A twist in the tale.

It must have been a long meeting because Kundan returned to his home/office at around 3 in the afternoon, where the entire crew of about a dozen people waited to hear about what happened.

Kundan smiled broadly and said,
"The script is through, no changes. I even had lunch with the advisor."
There were cheers all around.
"Why the hell didn't you call the office and tell us that the script was through?"
"I was enjoying my lunch."
"What did the advisor say?"

"He said that he had read the script thoroughly and gone through the comments of the script committee. He felt that if I heeded those comments it would destroy what I had."

"He said that?"

"His actual words were: 'Your script is like snow. If you make those changes, it will turn to ice.' He then called the Corporation and told them what he had told me. They accepted it. We are making the film with no changes."

There were cheers all around once more.

So what was the twist in the tale?

The 'script advisor' was my father. He had never met Kundan, nor had I talked about him when I visited my parents. When Kundan reached the Corporation office, he was given a note that had the name and address of the 'script advisor'. He realized it was my father, but he didn't tell me. They met each other independently, without any baggage.

The making of *Jaane Bhi Do Yaaro* would be a hilarious film in itself.

What Kundan was attempting to do in this film were two basic and contradictory things that could not be reconciled. If this would not cause havoc, what would? Simply put, his script was too long, the budget was too small.

Let me explain the problem a little more clearly. To shoot and edit the entire script would require a certain number of days. The budget that he had would allow him just two-thirds of that time. Since he was not going to cut down his script and his budget would not be increased, how the hell would he manage?

It was a crisis waiting to happen.

What transpired during the shoot and editing is the stuff of legends. Can anyone imagine how a film with these basic contradictions could be even completed? Kundan, along with two other stalwarts, his editor Renu Saluja and his co-writer and assistant director Sudhir Mishra, and the occasional 36-hour continuous shooting shift, made sure it was.

The net result was a great film where the budget was 'miraculously increased', shooting time was stretched to the point of cast and crew exhaustion, and almost one-third of what had been shot was left out in the editing bins.

The film did make a mark when it was released, but not as much as we had expected. Perhaps its political undertones, bizarre and sometimes absurd situations and cultural references made things a little difficult to digest. As time went by, its message and stance began to resound with newer generations and the film is considered a classic today. In fact, it is considered one of the hundred greatest films ever made in India.

.D.C. PRESENT
JAANE
BHI
DO
YAARO

A man transformed

There were subtle differences. He looked the same ... but. He walked the same ... but. He even talked the same ... but. Years ago, at film school, hadn't he talked of 'catching up', of gaining 'confidence'?

I think he had done so now ... and how!

Two memories.

The first: In late 1983, I was visiting a dilapidated housing colony that would be the main location for my third film. My brother Aziz, who was the production manager, had organized a trip to the site he had selected and Kundan, despite being busy on another project, joined us too. He just wanted to help out.

Twenty yards before we reached the site, we could smell it. The stench was overpowering and I had to cover my nose as I walked in from the main entrance. What we saw was absolutely horrific. Half-open sewers, garbage and filth dumped on the lower awnings, rats and cockroaches scurrying around the drains, some open, stinking toilets, electric wires hanging dangerously low, some attempts at repair half-done. This was not a dilapidated colony. This was a hell-hole left to rot.

It was in the heart of the city and that told you its story. It was deliberately allowed to decay by the landlord because he had no intention of doing any kind of repairs, and the tenants, unable to organize municipal assistance, were left to fend for themselves.

It was a waiting game: the landlord hoping for the tenants to leave so that he could reap windfall profits from the price of the land, and the tenants putting up a fight by not budging. The net result was a status quo and a living hell. But it was perfect for me. This was the story of my film. I knew I would have to spruce it up a bit, get some toilets cleaned and functioning, clear out some of the garbage and carry out a few repair jobs. Not too much though, because the 'look' was critical. Aziz was already working on the details and he had promised the tenants' association a generous amount to hire a lawyer to represent their case in court.

But a thought crossed my mind. The place would still be filthy because I had to have it that way. And though the stench would be reduced with a thorough scrubbing and cleaning, I knew it would never disappear. The years of neglect had seeped into the walls, floors, staircases, corridors.

I wasn't worried about my crew because I knew they would do their jobs no matter what the location. It was the actors that I was worried about. They would have to come here every day for ten days and for two whole nights. How would they react?

It was Kundan who sorted out my problem for me.

"Do you think this is the perfect location for your film?"
I nodded, and he continued.
"So what are you worried about? Do the actors come first or the film?"
Aziz smiled.
"Good question, Kundan."

That made up my mind. I would shoot here.

The second: Though my brother Aziz was the production manager for the film, Kundan would drop by to keep an eye on costs. He was Aziz's hatchet man and the one who pored over bills making sure there was no wastage of limited funds.

"Our job is that of a magician: we have to make every rupee into two."

I remember the time our production assistant, Pavan Malhotra, fresh from Delhi and also an aspiring actor, returned with a cheque from the Finance Corporation and Aziz asked:

"How did you get back so soon?"
Pavan hesitated a bit and then answered,
"I took a cab back."
"Why?" Kundan asked.
"The cheque was for a large amount. I was nervous about pickpockets on the train, so I ..."
That reply set Kundan off:

"So if you had got a cheque for a larger amount, would you have come by helicopter?"

Pavan got the message. Aziz laughed and added,
"Pavan, we can't afford cabs."

Kundan was back from England with a bang.

He was 'confident', he had 'caught up', and he had come home. This was also the time when he revealed the many mysteries of the 'sneaky bastards' to all of us, but there were other surprises awaiting him.

And there were body blows to come.

The first body blow

"What the hell is happening? Have we gone insane?" Kundan yelled.

This was his reaction when news started trickling in of the slaughter of Sikhs after the assassination of Indira Gandhi, India's Prime Minister. The assassination was bad enough, but this?

"What the f**k have ordinary Sikhs got to do with the killing?"
"I met a cab driver who had shaved his beard and cut his hair ... he was scared of being lynched."
Kundan shook his head in disbelief.
"And this is happening in Bombay! It must be hell in Delhi. In f*****g Sion, where I live, the people are talking about teaching 'them' a lesson. When I ask who is 'them', they mumble 'Sikhs' ... can you believe that? In f*****g Sion!"
"Welcome to the club, Kundan."
"What do you mean?"
"I was furious just like you when caste and communal riots took place in Gujarat, Maharashtra, in UP and Bihar, right through the 1960s, 70s, and now the 80s. It was Dalits and Muslims then, now it's the Sikhs."
"Are you saying I should not be outraged now ... that it is too late?"
"No, I am glad you are. We've been having these caste and communal riots for decades now ... but not enough people are outraged. If they were, these things would not happen ... so yes, f*****g get engaged with the world."

Kundan looked at me for a while, then said:
"Yeah ... I know. I realized that in England. When you get kicked in the ass, you learn a lot."
"That, my friend, is the tragedy ..."
"What do you mean?"
"Why do you have to have your personal ass kicked to realize things?"

Kundan nodded slowly.
"Sometimes it helps ... I'm sorry, but it's true for most people. But, what the hell is happening ... the assassination was bad enough, and now these killings in Delhi ... it's bloody madness! What were you saying about that Sikh cab driver?"

"He had to shave his beard and cut his hair to protect himself ... do you know what that means ...?"

Kundan shook his head and muttered:

"Where the hell have we reached?"

It is very late in the night. Everything seems to be so still. Almost all activities have come to a halt on the lake. Sitting alone on the patio of the houseboat, drink in hand, is an incredibly therapeutic experience. And it is now, thirty-seven years later, that I answer Kundan's question with another question.

Yes, Kundan, where the hell have we reached?

CHAPTER 10

The Partnership

It was television that brought us together. And for about twelve years, from 1984 to 1996, we had an extremely fruitful partnership that, for the first time, brought financial stability into our lives.

Yes, we loved films, but it was becoming increasingly difficult to survive with the returns we were getting. So Aziz, Kundan and I decided to check out the new and emerging world of television entertainment and programming. We formed a partnership that allowed us to go our separate ways with films but on the television front we were united.

The format worked. Aziz brought romance and music to the table, Kundan the passion, and I, the ideas. And in those twelve years we made a series of landmark television programmes that earned us very good financial returns. We were well set and we used this opportunity to create more programmes that we believed in ... that were more political, more edgy ... that tested the limits of what could be officially allowed on television.

Our office was buzzing with all kinds of activity. There were script-writing sessions, production meetings, scene rehearsals with actors, preparations for meals in the kitchen, and amidst all of this it was also the time when Kundan discovered the rat in the store-room.

I wasn't around when it happened, but when I reached the office people were talking about the event in whispers. It was the kind of stuff that would, over time, make history and the word would spread ...

Kundan "knew the psychology of rats".

This was also the time that he went on a book-buying spree. I gathered this piece of information because Bakula, his wife, complained that Kundan was spending what she thought was a fortune on books.

"He is just buying and buying. A whole cupboard is full."

And I also got a feel of what he was buying when he and I would have the following kind of conversation:

"I was reading Debiprasad Chattopadhyaya's *Lokayat*. I didn't know we had a long history of philosophical discourses on materialism. I thought we only had spiritual stuff."

"Yeah ... we've kept it a secret ... to make us think that we Indians don't believe in worldly things. It's a great way to maintain the status quo. This book is a people's history of India. It's about life and living."

"It was fascinating. I was also reading some essays by Noam Chomsky. Some of it is quite explosive ... on American foreign policy."

Or:

"I didn't know that Pablo Picasso was a communist."

"He was. And Charles Chaplin was branded as one too."

"I am aware of that. It seems that from the 1920s onwards there was a great cultural renaissance and upheaval around the world ... even in India. I was also reading about Bhagat Singh and Aurobindo ... Rash Behari Bose ... IPTA ... there was so much happening."

I could see that Kundan's reading habits were changing. From a large library of fiction and books on films and screenplays, he was now moving into the realm of history and art and from there on to the politics of art and further into political essays: Noam Chomsky, Edward Said, Romila Thapar, John Berger and Irawati Karve would enter his world. This world would include Karl Marx too ... but Kundan found reading him boring.

A funny tale.

Kundan Shah was going to Delhi because he had been appointed to be on the prestigious selection committee for the National Film Awards. This would require him to be in Delhi for a fortnight. So Bakula decided that he required a change of wardrobe befitting such an honour, and an amount of 8,000 rupees was given to Kundan to buy himself some shirts, trousers and jackets. It was a lot of money for those times.

Kundan set off with the cash and an unfortunate event occurred on the way. A couple of hundred yards before the readymade clothes market lay his favourite Mumbai bookshop: The Strand.

Kundan stopped by to browse but ended up spending the entire amount of money on books. The parcel was so heavy he had to take a taxi back home. Bakula was shocked as Kundan, by way of an explanation, told her:

"The screening of the films is going to be in a dark auditorium ... who is going to notice my clothes?"

Yes, those twelve years were years of plenty and we made full use of them. There was one hiccup though. One of our programmes ran into trouble. In fact, it ran into deep trouble.

We were producing a series on the workings of a police station and we decided to make seven episodes at one go. I still remember the hard work put in by Kundan, Aziz and Swaran Singh, the script writer. They spent months researching the project, weeks sitting at various police stations, observing and picking up stories from police personnel and undertrials. I also remember the effort and struggle of the cast and crew during the actual shoot.

The net result was a programme we were all proud of, with one caveat: I had a few reservations about the approach to the subject. It was extremely hard-hitting, and I thought that this would pose a problem with the authorities.

It did. They refused to pass the series, and Kundan and I decided to go to Delhi to fight our case. It was here that Kundan came into contact with a bunch of people who would thoroughly impress him, and a character named Javed Naqvi who would become a life-long friend.

The tale

We spent about a month in Delhi trying to convince the authorities to change their opinion about our programme. They in turn would call in their sets of 'experts' to opine on the whole affair, and in between these official meetings with the bureaucracy and experts and further promises of fresh deliberations, we had a lot of spare time on our hands.

We would often visit the office of the Communist Party of India (Marxist) where I had a few friends, and that was when Kundan began to meet the 'lefties': some real, some 'fellow travellers', some 'sympathizers', and some who could not make up their minds whether to be or not to be. They were writers, theatre people, teachers and musicians, journalists and painters, and we would sit on the lawn chatting about politics, history, music, art, literature, and also about the problems that Kundan and I were facing.

Kundan got a close look at them and realized that they also smiled and joked and laughed. They could be funny. They could be serious. They had families. Some were also vegetarians. 'Lefties' weren't too bad after all. Besides, they seemed to know a lot about a lot of things.

And then Kundan met Javed: the rebel with a cause.

Javed Naqvi, a graduate of the now 'targeted' Jawaharlal Nehru University, ex-member of the Students Federation of India, raconteur of tales and reciter of great poetry at the drop of a hat, was a wandering journalist in search of a newspaper, who had recently returned from an assignment in the Middle East.

He analysed our problem in a way it had never been done before.

"My dear friends," he proclaimed, "you are seeing the problem from a wrong point of view. You are seeing it as creators. But see it from the point of view of the state, which is the receiver of your creation. Then you will understand a lot of things."

He paused dramatically and then continued:

"The state is in deep shit. It has just about managed to stabilize the situation in Punjab after years of militancy, the assassination of a Prime Minister and horrible riots. And how has the state been stabilized? By tough police action. Cops are now the temporary kings of Punjab. It might not be democratic, but they are the kings. Then you have the Mandal Commission riots happening in Delhi and elsewhere. The BJP is threatening a *Rath Yatra* for the Ram temple. To control all these agitations you need cops. And what have you done?"

He paused again as a teacher would in a kindergarten class.

"You have screwed the cops. You have made them look like thugs ... which, under most circumstances, they are. So what choice does the state have? It is doing exactly what any state in deep shit would do. Protect the thugs who protect the state in deep shit.'

Kundan shook his head.
"So what should we do? Should we stop doing this kind of work because it might offend the state?"

"My dear fellow, your job is to create. And you would be a very bad creator if you did not offend somebody ... preferably the state. As Lord Krishna said, 'It is your dharma to create ... and to hell with the consequences.'"

Kundan smiled. He had made a friend for life.

Javed reveals a secret.

What no one noticed, but Javed did, was that for two whole days Kundan had skipped breakfast and lunch while we hung out on the lawn of the Party office. He even declined the tea that regularly made the rounds and the occasional glasses of water. That set Javed thinking. He took Kundan aside from the rest of us and probed. They spoke for a while and then Javed burst out laughing.

"What? ... I can't believe it!"

All of us turned to look at the two of them and Kundan seemed to be very embarrassed. Javed, being Javed, loudly announced:

"Friends and comrades ... I have an announcement to make! Our friend Mr Kundan Shah has been on a fast for the past two days and today is the third morning of his very private endeavour. The fast has two aspects to it: the first is a protest and the second is to atone for his sins."

He looked at Kundan and added: "Now, Mr Shah, will you please let these people know what you are up to?"

Acutely embarrassed, Kundan mumbled: "It was to be a very private fast. I just wanted to protest in some way about this whole affair ... for the freedom of speech. I did not know what else to do, so I ..."

Rajen Prasad smiled.

"So you decided to fast on the lawns of our office ...?"
"Where else could I do it?"
"Why didn't you tell us?"

"It was supposed to be private."
All of us looked at each other and tried to understand what he had just said. Then someone asked,

"What is the sin you are atoning for?"
"I should have listened to Saeed. He had warned me about the censors. I went a bit too far ... this serial cost us a lot of money, almost fourteen lakhs ... and I am responsible for it."

I smiled.

"Relax, I backed it too ... we made a great series ... we will recover the money from another one ..."

"So now will you have lunch?" Rajen asked.

Kundan nodded.
"I'm damned hungry ..."

We all laughed.

We spent another week in Delhi debating with the authorities and a milder version of the programme was reluctantly agreed upon by Kundan. But he was deeply bruised by the experience.

"They were real stories ... we did not invent them", he muttered. It was his first experience of how Power reacted to 'Truth'.

It was during those same days that we got to spend time with Javed and his wonderful wife Savita, both of whom gently nursed him. Javed with hilarious stories of his 'activism' as a student and poetry recitations, and Savita with some fabulous non-vegetarian meals in her home and the time to listen to Kundan's woes.

Kundan would talk about their hospitality and generosity for years.

The signs turn ominous.

Between 1986 and 1990 there were dark political clouds hovering over large parts of North India, and Kundan would experience the full force of politics and power.

As Javed had predicted, the pro- and anti-Mandal Commission agitations had turned violent with demonstrations across several towns and cities. To counter this political tactic, the Bharatiya Janata Party launched one of its own. It would soon embark on a massive road show, on a motorized chariot, across large parts of North India, calling on all Hindus to unite. They were going to build a grand temple in the town of Ayodhya on a piece of land which, they believed, was the exact spot where Lord Ram, the great Hindu god, was born.

The idea was combustible and frighteningly so, because the BJP had identified the exact spot of land on which, unfortunately, stood a medieval mosque. If this wasn't to be considered incendiary, what would be?

"How the hell can they identify that spot?" Kundan asked. "I was told that there are several *mandirs* in Ayodhya that claim to be on the exact spot where Lord Ram was born. This is getting ridiculous."

However a new crisis was emerging. In Kashmir elections were going to be held and a formidable political alliance had emerged that posed a serious threat to the traditional balance of power in the state. Judging by the massive and enthusiastic response this alliance was receiving, it seemed that many people in the Valley were fed up with the status quo and were looking for change. The battle lines were being drawn.

All these issues would gather momentum and by 1989 there was chaos across North India. I will start with Kashmir first.

The elections were held, and they were botched up and most probably rigged. Hundreds of thousands of Kashmiris protested and the state clamped down on them harshly. Hundreds upon hundreds were bludgeoned and tortured into submission. Protesting was not an option. That was when the militant movement began and across the border, an unfriendly neighbour welcomed angry and disillusioned young men from the Valley to train and arm them. Besides, it had hundreds of its own 'holy warriors' fresh from battles in Afghanistan to add to the mayhem that was now going to be unleashed in Kashmir.

Enough has been written about Pakistan's interference, but not enough of our own mishandling of the situation. We botched things too with our own political machinations and the harsh response to any form of dissent by a governor who, instead of healing wounds, added fuel to the fire. It was a double whammy, and two immense tragedies resulted from all these insidious political interventions.

The first was the forced departure of a very large number of Hindus from the Kashmir Valley. As things began to heat up, chilling Islamic slogans were raised in the night that frightened and alienated them. Then there was the targeted killing of Hindus, brutal murders actually, and most of it in the first two years. According to government sources, about 219 Hindus died in the insurgency. Some organizations believed it was almost double that figure.

However, what needs to be noted was that even in these scoundrel times of targeted minority Hindu murders, the number of Kashmiri Muslims who were also murdered in this period was far higher. They also paid a horrifying price and thousands of them migrated too. But the effect on the Hindus in such a situation was far graver, much more terrifying ... and mass migration of Kashmiri Hindus began in earnest. About 350,000 of them finally moved from the Valley to safer areas. They left behind everything ... including their history.

Could it be called ethnic cleansing? What else could one say if almost an entire people who had lived in this beautiful land for millennia, who had contributed so much to its cultural ethos, suddenly vanished? Very, very few Hindus would remain.

"It is going to leave a terrible scar," Kundan said. "Just imagine, you cannot trust your neighbours ... nothing can be worse than that ... neighbours for generations and then suddenly ..."

The second was the tragedy of the millions who were left behind in the Valley ... almost all of them Muslims. Trapped between the machinations of intelligence agencies, by militant groups sponsored from across the border and suspicious Indian armed forces who found it difficult to distinguish between a militant and a civilian, they have paid a horrible price: of humiliation and brutality, for more than thirty years.

Official figures put the total death toll to around 40,000 people. Others put it much, much higher. And that does not take into account the thousands upon thousands brutalized.

"It is a forsaken land. No one here gives a damn because most people living there are Muslims. That is the real truth."

Kundan could be blunt. But there was retaliation.
"What about the truth of the Hindus leaving the Valley?"
"Who the hell is condoning that? I said it was terrible ... but don't tell me that justifies what is happening in the Valley now."

... fools rush in ...

It was with this extremely complicated saga of deceit, duplicity, despair and death as the backdrop that in 2022, a film-maker with limited talent, unburdened by history or intelligence, decided to make and release a film on the 'story' of the Kashmiri Hindus. It was one-sided, shrill and jingoistic, and proved to be an incredible financial success as both the regime in power and the mainstream media backed and promoted his project with unbridled enthusiasm.

In all my life I have never seen such an overt coming together of the state, its nurtured intellectuals, its cultivated mainstream media and its stormtroopers, to promote such a piece of garbage, passing it off as the 'truth'.

In fact it was a travesty.

What the film-maker missed was the larger picture ... of a historical and political context ... of cause and effect in which an entire people, Kashmiri Muslim and Hindu, had been used as cannon fodder in the games played between cynical intelligence agencies, indoctrinated militants, fundamentalists of all hues, and the machinations of nations.

However, I must get back to Kundan.

He was also blunt about the Ram temple movement, which brings me to the second looming crisis.

"Do you really think the people will be fooled by these gimmicks? The bastards can't talk about economic issues, about hunger and unemployment, and education ... so they bring in God. *Kisko chutiye bana rahe hain*?"

But it worked. The movement had begun picking up incredible momentum and a lot of financial backing. Chilling slogans were being raised and people were being lynched along the path of the avenging motorized chariot. It didn't need great intelligence to figure out who these unfortunate people were.

"Isn't anybody noticing these deaths?" Kundan asked.

Nobody was. It all ended on the 6th of December, 1992, when hundreds of thousands of the faithful reached Ayodhya and a large group of them brought the mosque down. They were cheered and encouraged by some leaders of the BJP standing on a viewing platform close by.

"Just one more push", screamed a lady in saffron.

That push was given and down came the mosque, crushing a couple of the over-enthusiastic faithful. The leaders on the viewing gallery hugged each other. Kundan was dead wrong about people not being fooled by what he thought were inconsequential issues. In the next election, the BJP moved from a party of almost nothing to a party of plenty, and in this, a lesson was learnt: bigotry does pay dividends. It had paid dividends in Afghanistan too.

But I digress.

In the aftermath of the demolition of the mosque, my city, Mumbai, was burning. Communal riots had enveloped large sections of it and more than a thousand people would finally die. I recall one of the favourite slogans of the marauding mobs:

"The Muslim in India has just one choice: Pakistan or the graveyard."

As Kundan would say, "It was cute."

The violence didn't end however. A Muslim underworld thug decided to retaliate. A series of devastating bomb blasts would rip across the city that would take hundreds of innocent lives. Terror and counter-terror.

By 1995 our television odyssey was coming to a close. I would move on to make my fourth film, and Aziz would go on to make his first. Kundan in the meantime moved to his second, and this time into the world of mainstream cinema.

The film was an innovative experiment: a funny yet tragic love story where the protagonist is a mix between a charlatan and a besotted lover. Kundan was attempting to break new ground in the genre of romantic cinema. It did not quite work with the audiences, and in the making of it, Kundan did not forget to exhaust his cast and crew. He even got into a major spat with his producer who had tried to interfere in creative decisions.

However, along with cinema there were other things that caught his attention too. He had had a ringside seat to witness how politics could and would be used to manipulate frustration, anger and hate. He would also witness retribution.

In May 1991, Prime Minister Rajiv Gandhi was assassinated. It was the tragic culmination of a series of insidious political moves: of secretly arming and training a Tamil militia fighting for a separate homeland in Sri Lanka, of then working on a peace accord with the Sri Lankan government that didn't quite bring in the peace, then sending in the Indian army to fight the same guerrilla army it had trained, and finally, the insurgents sending in a suicide bomber to murder the Indian leader.

It was a reminder of how murky politics could be.

Then there was an upheaval that would shape the future, not just of India but of the world. It was the collapse of the Soviet Union. The Soviet Union had provided the rest of the world with a semblance of balance despite the fact that it did stomp around its zone of influence. That fragile balance was over and the United States of America was now the only remaining superpower. It would now have a free hand to stomp around the world wherever it wished. And stomp, it did.

And, with this state of affairs, Francis Fukuyama, the scholarly nitwit, would announce 'The end of History'.

But was it?

Snippet

"What did he mean by 'The end of History'?"

"I think he meant that there were no more obstacles and contradictions about how the world will be run. The philosophical debates are over ... there is no left or right ... the past is over and it will be smooth sailing from now on with the triumph of capitalism."

"Will it?"

"The man is a moron. He thinks socialism was an idea of the past and unfettered capitalism is the future. Greed and profit ... the world just got unbalanced a hell of a lot more."

"I predict total mayhem. The world is going to become one great casino."

"Yeah, the stock market is the new God ... now every right-wing moron is going to tell me how wrong I was ... that socialism belongs to the dust-bin of history ... with other bankrupt ideas."

"How the hell did the Soviet Union collapse so quickly?"

"I don't know. But my father said something that you will like. He said, 'It was an idea that had a lot of poetry in it ... and then, slowly, the poetry disappeared.'"

Sixteen years of change
Monica and Bill

and mayhem 1996–2012

These were sixteen years of incredible change in India and around the world: of terror attacks that led to wars, of countries devastated, horrendous revelations of torture and crimes against humanity, refugee crises of millions of people trying to flee their blighted lands, communal slaughter, genocide and ethnic cleansing, people's uprisings and violent suppressions, escalating terrorist atrocities around the world, suicide bombings and drone attacks, economic collapse, hunger and malnutrition, hope and despair, and spiralling seismic events that threatened to unhinge the world.

Kundan would call it *Zeitgeist* time ... time of the cabal and its machinations.

Zeitgeist was a film made by a man named Peter Joseph that was fundamentally a critique of market capitalism. Using a mixture of real history, a great deal of conjecture, some degree of the Marxist analysis of cause and effect, Joseph laid out his theory.

The film was in three parts. The first questioned the historicity of the Christian faith and the existence of Jesus by juxtaposing the religion with earlier myths and cults, and how a religion was born out of power play and by sleight of hand.

If that wasn't shocking enough, the second dealt with the terror attacks of 9/11, 2020. In this section the film went on to conjecture that the attack was an inside job, meant to launch the great WAR ON TERROR and basically reorganize the Middle East and also some other parts of the world. It was a battle for control of vital resources, to organize regime changes and to protect the interests of close allies in the region.

Whether it was true or not, the Middle East and North Africa were overhauled completely.

The third part was the critical one.

It was about a group of secretive bankers who controlled the Federal Reserve Bank of America, and through that, the almighty dollar. These were the men who really ran the world: they could create wars, organize chaos and mayhem, usher in their version of peace, control vital resources around the world and keep strict control over all forms of media information. And, to enforce their decisions, they were backed by a formidable military machine: the armed might of the United States of America.

This part of the film also backed up its arguments with examples of incidents that led to the USA joining the Second World War, its war with Japan thanks to a false flag operation at Pearl Harbor, and the Gulf of Tonkin incident that led to the Vietnam War.

Some of these arguments were based on hard facts ... others on inference and conjecture.

The net result was a conspiracy theory that was a powerful indictment of our scoundrel times.

Kundan was awed by the sheer sweep of the documentary. It covered all aspects of our lives: social, political, economic and religious, and it seemed to answer all the questions that he had about an iniquitous and unjust world. There was also an attempt at providing an alternative economic model that would redeem humanity from a system that, at its core, was run for profit and greed and endless consumerism.

In the midst of all of this Kundan would make four mainstream films and you could tell that his heart wasn't in them. Three failed at the box office and one wasn't released. Kundan decided to change track and do things his way.

He switched to the story of the three young sisters who had committed suicide in a small town in North India. This story, he felt, was more in keeping with the tumultuous events unfolding around him: the silent and personal tragedy of three young sisters who committed suicide to spare their lower-middle-class parents from the humiliation of finding them husbands. It was a true story and though I liked it, I did have quite a few reservations about Kundan's approach to the subject. I remember our heated arguments.

"What do you want me to do? Pander to the f*****g audience?"

"I am not saying that ... just make it a little more accessible to them. It's a tragedy that a lot of families go through ... it's their story too."

"Those young girls symbolize all that has f*****g gone wrong with our country ... all those brave words in our Constitution ... equality, the end of the caste system ... the film has to be austere, there can no space for any kind of relief ... I think the audience will understand."

"I hope so. I am glad you reduced the length of that monologue."

"Yeah, that is the only concession I made."

The film did not work. Kundan was deeply disturbed, but in a strange way he felt he had done what he had to do.

"I think it's an honourable failure", he muttered, and I agreed.

Then I added,
"By the way, I met Rahat Yusufi ..."

Kundan was surprised.
"When?"

"About a week ago ... on my way back from Goa."

"Why didn't you tell me?"

"You were busy with your film, so I felt ..."

Kundan nodded.
"How was he?"

"He seemed well. I don't think he wanted to meet up with his past."

Kundan smiled and muttered softly,

"That guy knows what our country is all about. He came from a privileged background ... and spent his f*****g life compensating for it."

Perhaps Kundan was right ...

What kept him riveted also were the political and economic events that were unravelling before him. There wasn't one of any significance that escaped his attention and to which he did not respond passionately. A few examples will explain what I am getting at.

He was incensed at the lies presented as evidence by the United States of America to the United Nations that led to the Iraq War, and finally to more than a million dead and millions of refugees:
"The Secretary of State of the United States of America is lying to the world at the United Nations! Can you believe that? It's a f*****g lie!"

He was outraged at the attempted coup to overthrow the elected government of Hugo Chavez in Venezuela:
"He was elected democratically by the people. But the West does not like that kind of democracy! So they try to overthrow him!"

He swore at Obama for bailing out the big banks and bankers who were behind the economic crash of 2008 where millions of ordinary people around the world faced ruin:
"Why is he bailing out those bastards! They should be in jail!"

But what stayed with me was his guilt at the communal massacre that occurred in Gujarat in 2002. All he could tell me was,

"I'm sorry, Saeed."

"What are you sorry about? This madness has nothing to do with you."

Kundan shook his head and muttered:

"You're wrong. You know why? Because no one is going to be held accountable ... no one! That's why I'm guilty. I am a Gujarati and a Hindu. Somebody has to take responsibility for what happened there."

I stared at him ... because I knew he was serious.

It was ironic that in the beginning of the twenty-first century, in the age of reason and rationality, Kundan had to reduce himself to being a Hindu and I, a Muslim. It said a lot about the times we were living in. And still are ...

So once again I ask:

Where the hell have we reached?

It was a miraculous sleight of hand.

How had a political party successfully convinced so many people that the problems of unemployment, malnutrition, poverty, education and health care, inequality, corruption, stifling of dissent and free speech, a manufacturing and farming crisis, police brutality, and the undermining of the autonomy of institutions including the judiciary were not the real issues facing our country ... and that the real problem lay elsewhere?

Sunset and whiskey time and Dr Strangelove 2012–2017

It was the end of the film and as the people trooped out of the preview theatre I could sense their bewilderment. They had just witnessed a cinematic installation that began when a prostitute falls in love with a corrupt and ambitious cop who manipulates her right through her tumultuous journey into the lurid world of politics, power, lust and greed.

That was the original idea, which sounded very reasonable and straightforward. Then why was the audience so bewildered?

It was because Kundan decided to turn this straightforward narrative into a bewildering circus of absurd and grotesque situations where whores, cops, judges, pimps, journalists, thugs, politicians, businessmen, industrialists and even wacky scientists play their part in preserving a system that fundamentally is a cancer that has corroded the entire political and social environment in India. And Kundan had underlined the idea ten-fold.

The only character left pure was the whore and her love. Everything else was completely contaminated.

Did the film work with the viewers leaving the preview theatre? I didn't think so. They mumbled their good wishes and appreciation with no eye contact and departed. Did it work for me? I don't know. I somehow felt that if there was a different cultural landscape in India, the film would have been received far more enthusiastically. But that's another story. Our cultural landscape had turned desolate.

It was sunset and whiskey time.

After the preview Kundan and I settled down for a drink at my home.

"It didn't work, did it?" he asked
"The audience seemed to be shocked ..."
"That was the purpose. One of the distributors asked why the film was so graphic and sometimes obscene."
"What did you tell him?"
"I asked him if it reflected the truth. The guy said, 'it did'. So I said, 'then why hide it?' I even told him that I had stopped short of making a porn film which would have been a closer reflection to the truth ... the guy was shocked."

He paused and then quietly added,
"I think my producer is confused too. I hope he doesn't feel that I let him down. I know my film lacks polish ... that's how it was meant to be. I now see the world as a *sadak chaap* and obscene tamasha ... an obscene circus ... does that make sense to you?"

I nodded.

"I think I should make porn films, but I have a question to ask you ..."
"What is it?"
"Is my cinema relevant?"
"You've made some shitty stuff ... and some stuff that is good ..."
"I know ... I keep experimenting. Have you seen Kubrick's *Dr Strangelove*?"
"I have ... I didn't quite like it."
"Why?"
"Cinema doesn't become good if it gets its politics right ... something more is needed."
"He was also seeing the nuclear world as a great tamasha ... a circus ... an obsession with power ... and destruction ... machismo."
"I know that ... but I think he was a bit simplistic."
"F**k you ... again a Marxist analysis."
"I thought you had forgiven us."

Kundan smiled, then continued:
"What's wrong with Kubrick's approach? There is an entire philosophy that celebrates war ... celebrates destruction ... sees the world in endless competition. Look at all the f*****g video games kids are playing nowadays ... they are hooked on to slaughter and mayhem ... that is what he is talking about. It's about the cabal."
"Nothing wrong with the analysis, but how the hell do you tell that story?"
"Yeah, maybe ... but I want to reach people, I want to engage with them. That's why I used the grotesque ... it doesn't seem to work. I keep trying, these thoughts keep coming to me ... I think I'm screwed up inside ..."
"We are all screwed up, Kundan ... don't think you are special. Now relax ... the film is over and done with."

Kundan thought that over, then finished his drink and left. The remark about 'porn' set me thinking. Was it a clue to understanding his work?

Kundan would get back to work on fresh ideas for other films, and twice a week we would meet in the evening for a drink. It could be at my home or his office, which were about two hundred yards apart. I preferred the meetings at home because Kundan served lousy whiskey in his office, which of course I never told him. I wish I had.

Unfortunately, he lost his office too.

In 2014, Bakula felt that the space would fetch far better returns if it was rented out and Kundan, realizing that perhaps his innings as a film-maker was over, quietly agreed. He would function out of home.

That must have hurt. The noisy get-togethers, discussions and debates would be a thing of the past. From then on Kundan would come to my place about twice a month and we would sit and chat about ideas that he was working upon and reflect upon the things we had done, could have done ... and whiskey seemed the perfect lubricant to fuel these reflections.

I remember the time we celebrated the anti-corruption campaign of Anna Hazare. Kundan, though in agreement with the agitation, added a note of caution.

"There is a lot of serious money behind this campaign ...where is it coming from?"

"That's true ... a lot of anti-Congress forces would be celebrating. But hasn't the movement struck a chord with people? Just look at the numbers flocking to those rallies!"

"Yeah ... it seems ordinary citizens want to see change."

We were following the campaign closely and it was our first real look at the 'gang' of people who were leading it.

Kiran Bedi we had dismissed as a flag-waving 'girl scout' cop. No depth. Just fervour. A person blissfully unaware of what her profession, the police force, had really become. It was an institution that by and large had been corroded by corruption, and had the dubious distinction of terrorizing the weak and the powerless. Most human rights reports testified to this fact. Kiran Bedi was perhaps clean, but was she aware of the stench that emanated from so many police stations and prisons around the country?

The other five drew our attention: Arvind Kejriwal, Prashant Bhushan, Yogendra Yadav, Manish Sisodia, Ashish Khetan.

"A good bunch", Kundan said.

So, when the Aam Aadmi Party was formed, we celebrated. When the leadership split, Kundan hit the roof.

"What the fuck are they doing?"
"The problem is that all of them have strong opinions."
"Isn't their goal the same?"

When the BJP swept the Lok Sabha elections in 2014, Kundan was depressed.

"Can't people see through their façade ... the lies?"
"My friend, you are seeing the magic of money and media power. Modi is the new messiah."

When the Aam Aadmi Party swept the legislature elections in Delhi a year later, Kundan was elated.

"What happened to the money and media power? What happened to the messiah? They tried every trick in the book ... religion, patriotism, war ... and they lost. It's a message to the country. These guys can be beaten!"

Then came a query:

"Can China and India really be friends ...?"

The question popped up because over the last six months Kundan had been reading up a lot about China. Was it really a threat to the US or was it an idea that gave America the leverage to pursue its strategic goals of military and technological superiority? Kundan felt that it was a great ploy ... to create a threat, then add words like 'freedom and democracy' and the argument turns potent. These two words had magical powers though no one knew what they really meant. On the other hand Kundan felt that if India could see through this 'game' it would be a breakthrough, and that is why the question popped up. I answered:

"I don't know. Whenever I think we can have some kind of rapport, we have these skirmishes on the border ... then we decide to flirt with the US ... that gets China riled ..."

"Yeah ... on the border we are vulnerable, that is a tragedy ... and the Americans know it. But here's the question: 'Why can't China see India as an equal partner?' Imagine that ... a counterbalance in Asia. Why does it view us as a potential threat?"

"We see them as a threat too ..."
"Yes, but what does China really want to be ... a superpower with all countries paying their *salaams*, or a friend of Asia ... what?"
"I'll ask Xi and let you know."
"F**k you!"

I laughed.

"Look, how the hell do I know what goes on in the minds of the Indian and Chinese think-tanks. As far as I'm concerned, we have just one bloody planet, that's all. It is damned stupid and childish to play 'I win, you lose' in such a situation. Geo-political thinking is a load of shit ... it just creates wars. Those people in think-tanks should all be sacked ... they are outdated. We need a complete overhaul of our economic and political thinking."

"What do you do about 'the cabal'?"
"Flushed down the toilet too."

Now Kundan laughed.

"That will be the day ... flushed down the toilet!"

Then there was the time when he made that classic announcement in my home.
I still remember it so clearly.
He had just entered and then casually said,
"I think I come from Scythian stock."
"What?"
Was he joking?
But he looked serious and repeated as he sat down.
"Scythian stock ... I read somewhere that quite a few people of Sindh and Gujarat have that ancestry ... it shows in their DNA."

I couldn't believe it.
"Scythian stock ... you? Have you seen yourself in the mirror?"
Kundan shrugged his shoulders.

"I could be an exception."
I kept silent and just stared at him. Was he really serious?

There was one evening however that really disturbed me. Kundan was in a different state of mind ... he was quiet, reflective ...

"Where do we go from here?" he asked.
"What do you mean?"
"Did you read that report about a man being lynched because he was suspected of eating beef?"
"Yes ... Mohammad Akhlaq."
"I think it's sick. There's another report about a Christian man being charged for blasphemy in Pakistan ... the clerics there are screaming for his head."
"I read that too ... those bastards don't waste any opportunity to bay for blood."
"What the hell is happening?" he said softly. "Just look at us ... we are heading into a crisis that everyone knows is coming and no one has the courage to talk about it. It's not just about this lynching ... the irony is that the cops took a sample of the meat in his fridge to have it checked, can you believe that? It turned out to be mutton ... but suppose it was beef, was the lynching then justified? It's f*****g crazy!"

"What is the crisis you are talking about?"

"A f*****g moral compass to distinguish between right and wrong ... we are losing it, my friend ... we are losing it."

"We lost it a long time ago. Picasso painted *Guernica* to remind us of the horrors of war ... the United Nations used it as a symbol for peace ... did it help?"

"That's not what I'm talking about. I am talking about people ... individuals and our moral compass ... there's too much hate floating around. If you kill and if you know you've done wrong ... that's the moral compass. If you kill and don't feel that ... you are not human. To take the life of an absolute stranger with no qualms, just because he believes differently ... we are going through that ... that is the crisis. Can I have another drink?"

"You can have dinner too ... I have beef in my fridge."

Kundan finally smiled.
"I'm going to report you to the cops."

That conversation was brutal. And that was the night that, for the first time, Kundan got drunk. Our get-togethers were about once a fortnight and Kundan would end up having about two or three drinks, rarely more. That night he hit the bottle as he talked about his differences with relatives, childhood friends and even neighbours. He was shocked.

"There is no outrage when I talk to them about what is happening ... they just stare at me, saying nothing. One neighbour even said 'they' had to be taught a lesson ... sometimes they even crack crude jokes."

As I heard him speak, I tried to calm him down. I tried telling him about the people I knew who did not think that way ... who were aware ... who understood what was happening and were trying to change things around. I talked to him about the hundreds of young and enthusiastic activists who were fighting this onslaught of hate ... didn't that matter?

"Too f******g few ... too few", he muttered. "There are hordes who think differently. You know, what is really disturbing is when they ask you why you are so disturbed. Relax, they say ... these things happen ..."

I had no answer to that.

The Celebration

There was, however, a silver lining in these dark times as Kundan arrived at my home one night with a broad smile on his face.

"Time to have a good drink", he said.

He had come to celebrate the rising tide of support for Bernie Sanders, the left-wing candidate for the Democratic Party in the upcoming US presidential election.

"Right now, an unapologetic socialist is the single most popular person in the United States of America. Can you believe that?"

"I can. For the first time the American people have got the opportunity to listen to what he stands for and they like it."

"Yeah ... decent education for all, affordable health care, raise the minimum wage, tax the rich, control the operations of banks and how big money influences elections ... the man has said everything and the people of America agree. They love it. On the streets of New York, the capital of the capitalist world, they are singing songs of protest. Can you believe that?"

"I can ... what a turnaround!"

Kundan smiled broadly.

"So tell all those right-wing morons that this is not 'The end of History'."

Then he turned serious.

"But I have a question for you ... will 'the cabal' allow him to win that Democratic Party nomination?"

I thought that over and said:

"They can't stop him. Every poll shows him beating Hillary Clinton. The people are on his side. Look at the crowds he is generating!"

But.

Stop him they did. In a strange twist to the electoral process, Bernie Sanders was stopped. Hillary Clinton was elected the Democratic Party candidate. She went on to be defeated by Donald Trump, a rabble-rouser who had said: "Clean the swamp." Hillary Clinton was the swamp. She represented the power elite in Washington, big banks and big business. What people didn't realize was that Donald Trump was part of the swamp too.

A thought.

It is strange that I felt so elated with the arrival of Bernie Sanders on the

American political scene. After years of a world media onslaught deriding the ideas of what socialism stood for, of actually making words like equality and justice sound like cliches, of making the collapse of the Soviet Union an example of a failed political and economic philosophy, Bernie Sanders erupted in the heart of the counter-narrative. He erupted in the land of the free, the brave and democratic, and told the people that they were not really free, nor their system really democratic.

It was actually a society of, for and by the powerful.

And in this heart of the 'free and democratic' world, his words resonated with the people and they stood by him in the millions. Millions upon millions. He, as an individual, was the most popular politician in the United States of America and, most importantly, he called himself a democratic socialist. Actually he proclaimed it ... and the people of America accepted it.

I felt good. But I must get back to Kundan.

A last meeting

After a long evening of the two of us analysing films, literature and art, Kundan was at the door of my apartment and about to depart. The elevator had arrived when suddenly he decided to start a new conversation.

"You know Saeed, wouldn't it be funny if we could record a private conversation between Donald Trump and Modi? ... I think it would be damned funny."

"Why?"

"One of them claiming to be the leader of the world's greatest democracy and the other of the world's largest ... isn't that funny? Try and imagine a film about them discussing this issue, about democracy ... it would be surreal. The greatest versus the largest, both of them cheerleaders for their country ... what a farce, I was thinking ..."

That was when I interrupted him.

"When do you stop thinking, Kundan? Go home ... I'm bloody tired."

Kundan quietly nodded.

"Yes, I guess it's late."

He got into the elevator and left. Two days later I departed for Goa. It was there that I found out that he had died.

It was like a body blow ... I felt numb. And so many years later, I still do. Sometimes, to cheer myself up, I imagine him having heated discussions with 'heavenly powers' about the inequities on earth. It makes me smile.

You know something Kundan?
That last meeting haunts me and I keep asking myself,
why the hell didn't I let you finish what you had to say?
It would have been great to hear your take on that conversation.
Alas ...

a song in memory

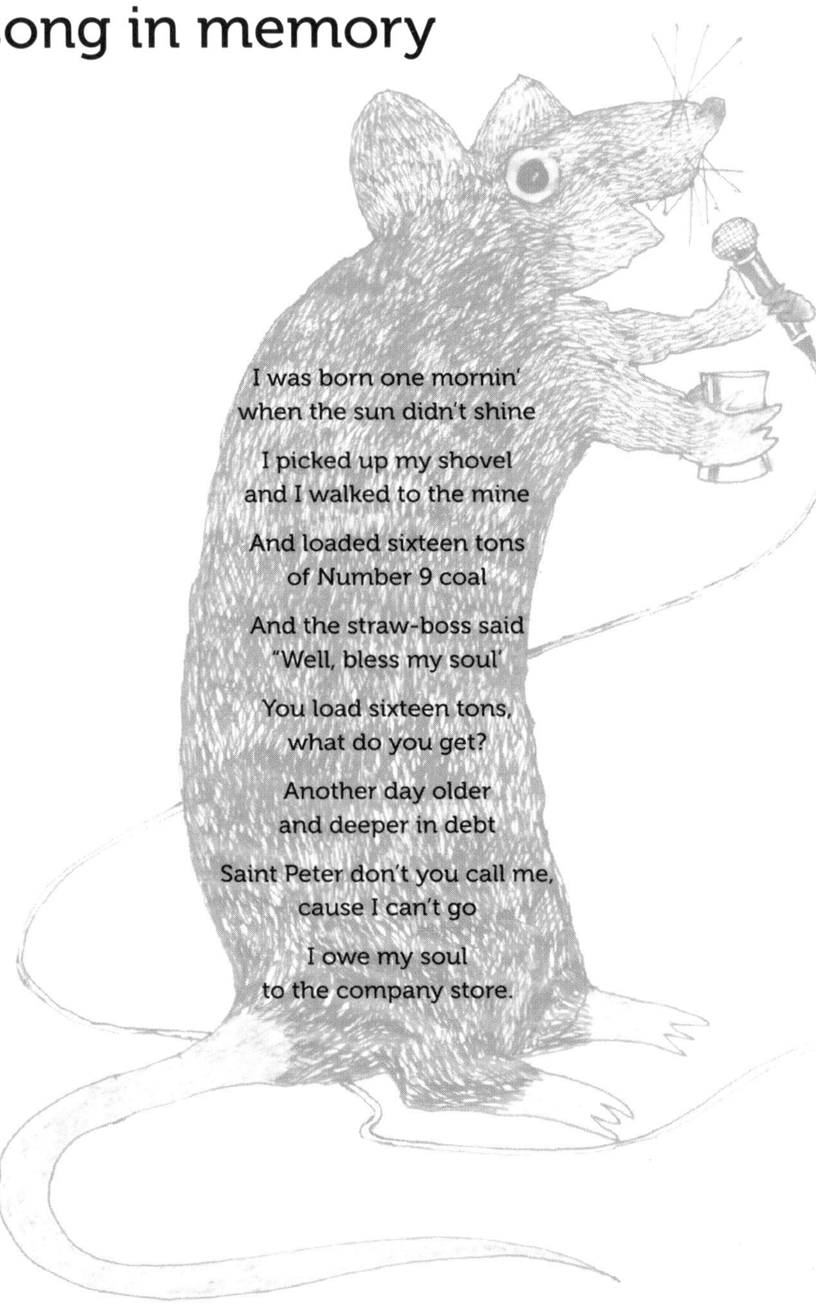

I was born one mornin'
when the sun didn't shine

I picked up my shovel
and I walked to the mine

And loaded sixteen tons
of Number 9 coal

And the straw-boss said
"Well, bless my soul'

You load sixteen tons,
what do you get?

Another day older
and deeper in debt

Saint Peter don't you call me,
cause I can't go

I owe my soul
to the company store.

Lyrics of the protest song 'Sixteen Tons' that Kundan loved to hear me sing. It was a song that I picked up in the late 1950s and embarrassed my sons by singing it at family get-togethers. It was also sung by activists in the Occupy Wall Street movement in New York from 2008 to 2010.

Soliloquy 4

I sit on the houseboat and think: this is the end, my friend.

We had a great innings together and now it's over.

But I am not done yet.

I have a mission to accomplish.

I have to have a conversation with the people of my country and nail one last lie.

There is a new narrative that is rapidly sweeping across my land. It is the story about a distant past where a great civilization existed in peace and harmony until a barbarous band of invaders destroyed it by marauding and pillaging this incredibly unique nation. A superior people ravaged by savages that led to a thousand years of slavery.

It is a narrative of the past that allows its believers so many insidious possibilities for the present. It divides people: Us and Them. The patriot and the fifth columnist. It allows for hate, it allows for demonization of a religion and, if one stretches the argument, it even allows for retribution. It could be converted to payback time. With no guilt. No shame. And no remorse.

This was a classic example of the weaponization of history and every fascist loves it.

However.

This narrative is an insult to my intelligence. Besides, it is also a lie.

I will now list out the names of some of the kingdoms and empires that existed and disappeared before the coming of these 'outsiders': the Cholas, Cheras, Pandyas, Chalukyas, Hoysalas, Shungas, Palas, Pratiharas, Kakatiyas, Satvahanas, kingdoms in Kashmir, Gujarat and Sindh, Yadavas, Gonds, Solankis, Kalinga, Nandas, Magadh, Kannauj, Mathura, Kashi, Rashtrakutas, Pallavas, Gauds, the Mauryas, the Guptas and the Kushans.

Now, one simple question needs to be asked: How did one kingdom or empire give way to another? Was it over a cup of tea and biscuits or the spilling of blood?

So what is the story?

There is enough evidence in Hindu, Buddhist and Jain literature and tales to tell you that there were wars, carnage, plundering and desecration. There was a lot of spilling of blood as empires changed and kingdoms collapsed. One shudders at the story of Ashoka's violent ascent to power or Parashuram's revenge against the Kshatriyas. Of the carnage that warriors like Pushyamitra and Shashanka wreaked. Of the mayhem recorded in the Mahabharata. That's what wars are all about and that is how kingdoms change and empires fall.

That is not all.

Hindu kingdoms fought against other Hindu kingdoms, Shaivites against Vaishnavites and also against Buddhist and Jain empires. They even destroyed each other's places of worship. The history of the Shunga, Pala, Gaud and Rashtrakuta empires reveals bloody massacres and desecrations. Yes, there was bigotry too. Places of worship were destroyed and people were killed for their beliefs. There is the classic story of a king offering a bounty for the head of every Buddhist slaughtered.

Yes, the past was not all that tranquil and peaceful as it is made out to be.

One should not be surprised by all of this because it is how empires are created, extended, controlled and then destroyed. The wily Chanakya revealed so many secrets in his writings on 'state-craft'.

Does all this mean that the Indian civilization before the coming of the Afghans and Turks was not great? No. It simply means that this sophisticated confluence of ideas, cultures and philosophies also spilt a great deal of blood.

I shall now come to the 'barbarous invaders'.

Yes, they did invade and they fought against Hindu kingdoms and empires. They did desecrate and destroy temples. They came as iconoclasts and they behaved as such. Were they biased towards people of their own faith? Of course, they were. Can you imagine this age as being democratic and just? Was it just before their arrival?

Once established, however, things began to change as they made alliances with Hindu kings and chieftains, had Hindu administrators, financiers, and their scholars, doctors, scribes, musicians, administrators, historians, poets, architects and sufis began to mingle and to learn from this ancient land. Songs began to be sung together, festivals celebrated together. And would love and poetry be far behind? Yes, as much as this civilization honoured war and valour, it celebrated love, literature and poetry too. Along with these interactions and over time, a new strand of colour was being added to a large, existing canvas.

The new entrants fought among themselves too, and dynasties changed from the Tughlaq to the Slave to the Khiljis and the Lodis. These Sultans also confronted the Mongol hordes and faced the wrath of Timur, both Muslim armies from the north and west.

Was everything perfect? No. Was there a lurking hostility to these new arrivals? Were there cases of injustice and bigotry? There must have been. But beyond that, imperial power had the capacity of forming close friendships, alliances and marriages too.

Finally, 'the children of Babar' arrived. This was the term used by these purveyors of false histories to describe the Mughal empire. The question is, who the hell did the Mughals really fight?

Yes, Babar did fight a couple of Rajput kings, but his biggest battles were against the Muslim Afghans: the earlier rulers. All through the reigns of the Mughals till the time of Aurangzeb, their greatest enemies were other Muslim kingdoms – in Gujarat, Sindh, Punjab, Kandahar, Kabul, Malwa – and Muslim usurpers in Bihar and Bengal. What is important to note is that it was a Muslim Mughal and Hindu Rajput alliance, which included marriages and children that had created the empire.

Another 'truth': this alliance slaughtered Muslims and Hindus in equal measure, and, if one goes by the rules of the game, it was quite ghastly. All wars are.

As we move to the South, the biggest obstacle to Mughal dominance were the Deccan sultans whose commanders and chiefs were either Abyssinian warriors, Marathas or Andhras. To these kingdoms the Mughals were the outsiders; over more than three hundred years, from the fourteenth to the seventeenth centuries, a distinct Persian, Andhra and Maratha culture had taken shape in these lands, and hundreds of Hindus were important administrators, nobles and commanders. There were many alliances through marriages too.

Does anybody know that Shivaji's grandfather, Maloji Bhonsle, was a commander under the Abyssinian Sultan Malik Amber? Does anyone know that the two were brilliant warriors and perfected the art of guerrilla warfare as they confronted the Mughal armies of Emperor Jehangir? Does anyone know that this same grandfather went to the mausoleum of a sufi saint named Shah Sharif to pray for male children? Does anyone know that when those heirs were born they were named Shahji and Sharifji after that same sufi saint?

Yes, the Muslim Mughals did fight against the Muslim Sultans, but so many of their commanders were Hindus. The Muslim Sultans fought the Muslim Mughals and many of their commanders were Hindus too. To add to this confusion many Hindu kings had Muslim commanders and soldiers in their armies – so who was fighting who?

There is the famous case of Maharana Pratap confronting the forces of Emperor Akbar at the battle of Haldighati. Of his two commanders, one was a Muslim, and his army of three thousand comprised a thousand Afghan warriors. Do people know about this little detail? On the other hand, was Emperor Akbar leading his army? No. It was led by Man Singh, a Hindu general.

As an aside, I would like to add that numerous wives and concubines were not just a phenomenon of 'degenerate' Muslims. A great number of Andhra, Rajput, Sikh and Maratha kings and nobles had wives and harems too. In fact Chhatrapati Shivaji had six wives. Does that make him less of a hero? No. He was a great king and warrior of his times.

The question that needs to be asked of these purveyors of false histories is: Why have they left these little details hidden? What purpose does it serve and who benefits from it?

Let me guess.

I believe the seven hundred years of Islamic influence did two basic things. It completely undermined the role of Sanskrit as a power base. But more important than that was the rapid expansion of vernacular languages: Hindivi, Braj, Khadi Boli, Awadhi, Bengali, Gujarati, Deccani, Urdu, Marathi, Telugu, Kannada ... The practitioners of 'high culture' would be aghast at this subaltern intrusion. The second was the rise of the Sufi and Bhakti movements which, at their core, critiqued mindless rituals, and attacked the pompousness and hypocrisy of clerics and priests. Try and imagine these 'worthy' personages being ridiculed. After centuries of glorification and impunity, what would their reaction be?

Having said this, I must get back to my argument about empires.

As far as the growth of the Maratha and Sikh empires is concerned, their biggest battles and conquests occurred after the death of Aurangzeb. After him the empire began to falter ... and the old order was changing rapidly with the rise of the Marathas and the sacking of Delhi by Nadir Shah, the Persian Sultan. By 1740 the Mughal empire had been hollowed out, emptied. It remained Mughal only in name. The really big guns were the Marathas and the Sikhs. There were some reviving Rajputs, Gujjars, Jats and the sultans of Bengal and the kingdoms of the South. Did they plunder, maraud and kill as they extended their empires? They did. Waiting in the wings and gaining strength were the British as they played one power against the other.

In fact, from 1740 onwards it was a free-for-all. And finally, one by one, almost all of them genuflected to the British raj. Sikh, Maratha, Muslim, Rajput, Jat, the Nizam and the kingdoms of the South. All of them prostrated. Except perhaps one. He died in the battlefield fighting them. Guess who it was.

So, was Mughal rule perfect? No. Were there cases of intolerance and bigotry? I am sure there were. As I said earlier, as with all feudal empires, there was anguish and injustice too. The important point to note was that Hindus and Muslims fought together and also against each other.

Therefore, the idea of seven hundred years of history of Muslims on one side and Hindus on the other is an insult to my intelligence. The idea that only Muslims can be violent, cruel, and plunder and kill is an insult to my intelligence. The idea that Hindus are non-violent and peaceful is another piece of garbage. As the saying goes:

"*Hammam mein sab nange hain.*"
(Everyone is naked in the public baths.)

Some more points to note: These 'invaders' never left. They lived and died and are buried right here, in this land. Generations upon generations of their graves are testament to this simple truth.

They created exquisite monuments and palaces, built public buildings and laid out gracious cities, they built courts, hospitals, markets, caravan serais and ports for trade, and enriched the land with music, literature and tales, food, language, dress codes, poetry, architecture and gardens. They also built an administrative structure across the land that exists till today. And, most importantly, they did not stash their wealth abroad as so many 'patriots' do today.

Will all of this convince these writers of false histories? Frankly, I don't know, and I don't give a damn. They are born in hate, they lack humour and, most importantly, they have no poetry in their souls.

So let them create their narratives of the past, create history to suit their ideological needs because they have the numbers in Parliament.

But, as Kundan would say,

"If ten guys say you are drunk, don't lie down. Stand up and speak out."

Yes, Kundan ...
the battle has been joined.

Snippet

"Remember that scene in *The Great Dictator* where Charlie Chaplin plays with that plastic globe? Remember how he kicks and flicks it around?"

"Yes ..."

"He seemed to be having a great time. Sometimes I wish we could do the same thing ... shake things up in our screwed-up world to get some kind of equilibrium."

"By having fun kicking a plastic globe around?"

"No, kicking the real world around ..."

I laughed at the idea. He laughed too.

"You're nuts!" I said.